Deep Learning with Microsoft Cognitive Toolkit Quick Start Guide

Practical guide to building neural networks using Microsoft's open source deep learning framework

Willem Meints

BIRMINGHAM - MUMBAI

Deep Learning with Microsoft Cognitive Toolkit Quick Start Guide

Copyright © 2019 Packt Publishing

Commissioning Editor: Amey Varangaonkar
Acquisition Editor: Siddharth Mandal
Content Development Editor: Mohammed Yusuf Imaratwale
Technical Editor: Jane D'souza
Copy Editor: Safis Editing
Project Coordinator: Kinjal Bari
Proofreader: Safis Editing
Indexer: Tejal Daruwale Soni
Graphics: Alishon Mendonsa
Production Coordinator: Jisha Chirayil

First published: March 2019

Production reference: 1260319

Published by Packt Publishing Ltd.
Livery Place
35 Livery Street
Birmingham
B3 2PB, UK.

ISBN 978-1-78980-299-3

www.packtpub.com

To my wife – she always makes me smile, no matter where we are.
To my two little neural networks, also known as my sons, Tom and Luuk.

`mapt.io`

Mapt is an online digital library that gives you full access to over 5,000 books and videos, as well as industry leading tools to help you plan your personal development and advance your career. For more information, please visit our website.

Why subscribe?

- Spend less time learning and more time coding with practical eBooks and Videos from over 4,000 industry professionals

- Improve your learning with Skill Plans built especially for you

- Get a free eBook or video every month

- Mapt is fully searchable

- Copy and paste, print, and bookmark content

Packt.com

Did you know that Packt offers eBook versions of every book published, with PDF and ePub files available? You can upgrade to the eBook version at `www.packt.com` and as a print book customer, you are entitled to a discount on the eBook copy. Get in touch with us at `customercare@packtpub.com` for more details.

At `www.packt.com`, you can also read a collection of free technical articles, sign up for a range of free newsletters, and receive exclusive discounts and offers on Packt books and eBooks.

Contributors

About the author

Willem Meints is a software architect and engineer with a wide variety of interests. His background in software engineering hasn't stopped him from exploring new areas, such as machine learning, as part of his daily work. This sparked a deep passion for everything related to artificial intelligence and deep learning.

Willem studied electronics after his high school career, but quickly discovered he had more fun building applications. This led to his decision to leave the world of electronics and launch a career in software engineering. After he finished his bachelor's degree in software engineering, he started working for Info Support, where he's been working ever since.

About the reviewer

Bahrudin Hrnjica holds a PhD in technical science from the University of Bihać. Currently, he is assistant professor at the university, teaching students in the fields of numerical analysis, mathematical modeling, and machine learning. Besides teaching at the university, he has many years' experience in the software industry, working on custom solutions based on cloud technologies, machine learning, .NET, and Visual Studio. As an expert in development technologies, Microsoft recognized him as Microsoft Most Valuable Professional (Microsoft MVP) for the first time in 2011. He is an author of several books, online articles, and open source projects, as well as having spoken at many local and regional conferences, code camps, and workshops.

Packt is searching for authors like you

If you're interested in becoming an author for Packt, please visit `authors.packtpub.com` and apply today. We have worked with thousands of developers and tech professionals, just like you, to help them share their insight with the global tech community. You can make a general application, apply for a specific hot topic that we are recruiting an author for, or submit your own idea.

Table of Contents

Preface

Artificial intelligence (**AI**) is here to enhance humans by automating some of the tasks we do every day, so we can spend more time fully realizing our potential. We've been using software programs as tools to automate many of the simpler tasks. Now it is time to take on the challenge of automating more complicated tasks.

There's a lot happening in the area of AI and more people than ever are looking to expand their existing toolkit with new techniques to make their software smarter. Machine learning, and especially deep learning, are highly important tools with which we can enhance what we are already doing with our computers.

This book aims to help you get to grips with one of the most popular deep learning tools, CNTK. We will look at what this relatively young open source deep learning framework offers. At the end of this book, you'll have a solid understanding of the framework and some of the scenarios in which it can be used.

Who this book is for

This book is great for developers with some experience in Java, C#, or Python. We're assuming you're pretty new to machine learning. However, this book is also great for people who have worked with other deep learning frameworks before and want to learn another great deep learning tool.

What this book covers

Chapter 1, *Getting Started with CNTK*, introduces you to the CNTK framework and the world of deep learning. It explains how to install the tools on your computer and how to use a GPU with CNTK.

Chapter 2, *Building Neural Networks with CNTK*, explains how to build your first neural network with CNTK. We dive into the basic building blocks and see how to train a neural network with CNTK.

Chapter 3, *Getting Data into Your Neural Network*, shows you different methods of loading data for training neural networks. You'll learn how to work with both small datasets, and datasets that don't fit in your computer's memory.

Chapter 4, *Validating Model Performance*, teaches you how to work with metrics to validate the performance of your neural network. You'll learn how to validate regression models and classification models and what to look for when trying to debug your neural network.

Chapter 5, *Working with Images*, explains how to use convolutional neural networks to classify images. We'll show you the building blocks needed to work with spatially-ordered data. We'll also show you some of the most well-known neural network architectures for working with images.

Chapter 6, *Working with Time Series Data*, teaches you how to use recurrent neural networks to build models that can reason over time. We'll explain the various building blocks that you need to build and validate a recurrent neural network yourself, based on a IoT sample.

Chapter 7, *Deploying Models to Production*, shows you what it takes to deploy deep learning models to production. We'll take a look at a DevOps environment with a **continuous integration/continuous deployment (CI/CD)** pipeline to teach you what it takes to train and deploy models in an agile engineering environment. We'll show you how you can use a tool such as Azure Machine Learning service to take your machine learning efforts to the next level.

To get the most out of this book

We recommend you have experience with Python 3 so that you know what the syntax looks like. You will need to run either Linux or Windows on a machine with a decent amount of memory and CPU power, as the samples in this book can take a long time to run on an older machine. If you are lucky enough to have a gaming graphics card in your machine from NVIDIA, we definitely recommend looking at the instructions on how to install the GPU version of CNTK, as this can speed up the samples by quite a large factor. Some sections in the book assume that you know a little bit about Java or C#. Although not required, it is useful to have a basic understanding of the syntax of one or more of these languages.

Download the example code files

You can download the example code files for this book from your account at www.packt.com. If you purchased this book elsewhere, you can visit www.packt.com/support and register to have the files emailed directly to you.

You can download the code files by following these steps:

1. Log in or register at www.packt.com.
2. Select the **SUPPORT** tab.
3. Click on **Code Downloads & Errata**.
4. Enter the name of the book in the **Search** box and follow the onscreen instructions.

Once the file is downloaded, please make sure that you unzip or extract the folder using the latest version of:

- WinRAR/7-Zip for Windows
- Zipeg/iZip/UnRarX for Mac
- 7-Zip/PeaZip for Linux

The code bundle for the book is also hosted on GitHub at https://github.com/PacktPublishing/Deep-Learning-with-Microsoft-Cognitive-Toolkit-Quick-Start-Guide. In case there's an update to the code, it will be updated on the existing GitHub repository.

We also have other code bundles from our rich catalog of books and videos available at https://github.com/PacktPublishing/. Check them out!

Code in Action

Visit the following link to check out videos of the code being run:
http://bit.ly/2UcIfSe

Conventions used

There are a number of text conventions used throughout this book.

CodeInText: Indicates code words in text, database table names, folder names, filenames, file extensions, pathnames, dummy URLs, user input, and Twitter handles. Here is an example: "We use the StreamDef class for this purpose".

A block of code is set as follows:

```
from cntk.layers import Dense
from cntk import input_variable

features = input_variable(50)
layer = Dense(50)(features)
```

Any command-line input or output is written as follows:

```
cd ch2
jupyter notebook
```

Bold: Indicates a new term, an important word, or words that you see onscreen. For example, words in menus or dialog boxes appear in the text like this. Here is an example: "To create a new instance of this resource type, click the **create** button."

 Warnings or important notes appear like this.

 Tips and tricks appear like this.

Get in touch

Feedback from our readers is always welcome.

General feedback: If you have questions about any aspect of this book, mention the book title in the subject of your message and email us at customercare@packtpub.com.

Errata: Although we have taken every care to ensure the accuracy of our content, mistakes do happen. If you have found a mistake in this book, we would be grateful if you would report this to us. Please visit www.packt.com/submit-errata, selecting your book, clicking on the Errata Submission Form link, and entering the details.

Piracy: If you come across any illegal copies of our works in any form on the Internet, we would be grateful if you would provide us with the location address or website name. Please contact us at copyright@packt.com with a link to the material.

If you are interested in becoming an author: If there is a topic that you have expertise in and you are interested in either writing or contributing to a book, please visit authors.packtpub.com.

Reviews

Please leave a review. Once you have read and used this book, why not leave a review on the site that you purchased it from? Potential readers can then see and use your unbiased opinion to make purchase decisions, we at Packt can understand what you think about our products, and our authors can see your feedback on their book. Thank you!

For more information about Packt, please visit `packt.com`.

Getting Started with CNTK 1

Deep learning is a machine learning technique that is getting a lot of attention from the public and researchers. In this chapter, we will explore what deep learning is and how large companies are using it to solve complex problems. We'll look at what makes this technique so exciting and what concepts drive deep learning.

We will then talk about **Microsoft Cognitive Toolkit** (**CNTK**), what it is, and how it fits into the bigger picture of deep learning. We'll also discuss what makes CNTK unique compared to other frameworks.

In this chapter, we'll also show you how to get CNTK installed on your computer. We will explore installation on both Windows and Linux. If you have a compatible graphics card, you'll also want to check out the instructions on how to configure your graphics card for use with CNTK, as it will significantly speed up the calculations that are needed to train deep learning models.

In this chapter we will cover the following topics:

- The relationship between AI, machine learning, and deep learning
- How does deep learning work?
- What is CNTK?
- Installing CNTK

The relationship between AI, machine learning, and deep learning

In order to understand what deep learning is, we have to explore what **Artificial Intelligence** (**AI**) is and how it relates to machine learning and deep learning. Conceptually, deep learning is a form of machine learning, whilst machine learning is a form of AI:

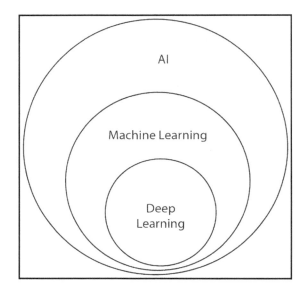

In computer science, Artificial intelligence, is a form of intelligence demonstrated by machines. AI is a term that was invented in the 1950s by scientists doing research in computer science. AI encompasses a large set of algorithms that shows behavior that is more intelligent than the standard software we build for our computers.

Some algorithms demonstrate intelligent behavior but aren't capable of improving themselves. One group of algorithms, called machine learning algorithms, can learn from sample data that you show them and generate models that you then use on similar data to make predictions.

Within the group of machine learning algorithms there's the sub-category of deep learning algorithms. This group of algorithms uses models that are inspired by the structure and function of a biological brain found in humans or animals.

Both machine learning and deep learning learn from sample data that you provide. When we build regular programs, we write business rules by using different language constructs, such as if-statements, loops, and functions. The rules are fixed. In machine learning, we feed samples and an expected answer into an algorithm that then learns the rules that connect the samples to the expected answers:

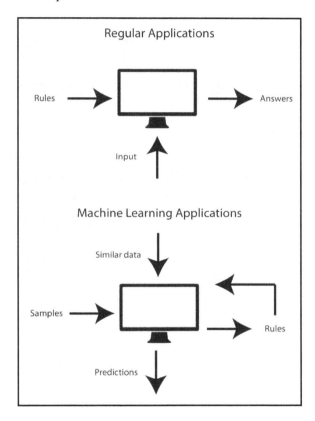

There are two major components in machine learning: machine learning models and machine learning algorithms.

When you use machine learning to build a program, you first choose a machine learning model. A machine learning model is a mathematical equation containing trainable parameters that transforms input into a predicted answer. This model shapes the rules that the computer will learn. For example: predicting the miles per gallon for a car requires that you model reality in a certain way. Classifying whether a credit card transaction is fraudulent requires a different model.

The representation of the input could be the properties of a car turned into a vector. The output of the model could be the miles per gallon for a car. In the case of credit card fraud, the input could be the properties of the user account and the transaction that was done. The output representation could be a score between 0 and 1 where a value close to 1 means that the transaction should be rejected.

The mathematical transformation in the machine learning model is controlled by a set of parameters that need to be trained for the transformation to produce the correct output representation.

This is where the second part, the machine learning algorithm comes into play. To find the best values for the parameters in the machine learning model we need to perform a multi-step process:

1. Initially, the computer will choose a random value for each of the unknown parameters in your model
2. It will then use sample data to make an initial prediction
3. This prediction is fed into a `loss` function together with the expected output to get feedback regarding how well the model is performing
4. This feedback is then used by the machine learning algorithm to find better values for the parameters in the model

These steps are repeated many times to find the best possible values for the parameters in the model. If all goes well, you end up with a model that is capable of making accurate predictions for many complicated situations.

The fact that we can learn rules from examples is a useful concept. There are many situations where we can't use simple rules to solve a particular problem. For example: credit card fraud cases come in many shapes and sizes. Sometimes a hacker slowly breaks the system injecting smaller hacks over time and then stealing the money. Other times hackers simply try to steal a lot of money in one attempt. A rule-based program would become too hard to maintain because it would need to contain a lot of code to handle all different fraud cases. Machine learning is an elegant way to solve this problem. It understands how to handle different kinds of credit card fraud without a lot of code. And it is also capable of making a judgment on cases that it hasn't seen before, within reasonable boundaries.

Limitations of machine learning

Machine learning models are very powerful. You can use them in many cases where rule-based programs fall short. Machine learning is a good first alternative whenever you find a problem that can't be solved with a regular rule-based program. Machine learning models do, however, come with their limitations.

The mathematical transformation in machine learning models is very basic. For example: when you want to classify whether a credit transaction should be marked as fraud, you can use a linear model. A logistic regression model is a great model for this kind of use case; it creates a decision boundary function that separates fraud cases from non-fraud cases. Most of the fraud cases will be above the line and correctly marked as such. But no machine learning model is perfect and some of the cases will not be correctly marked as fraud by the model as you can see in the following image.

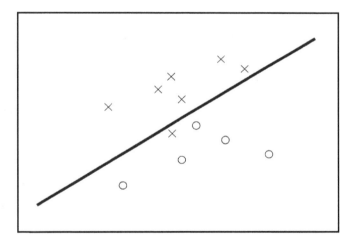

If your data happens to be perfectly linearly-separable all cases would be correctly classified by the model. But when have to deal with more complex types of data, the basic machine learning models fall short. And there are more reasons why machine learning is limited in what it can do:

- Many algorithms assume that there's no interaction between features in the input
- Machine learning are, in many cases, based on linear algorithms, that don't handle non-linearity very well
- Often, you are dealing with a lot of features, classic machine learning algorithms have a harder time to deal with high dimensionality in the input data

How does deep learning work?

The limitations discovered in machine learning caused scientists to look for other ways to build more complex models that allowed them to handle non-linear relationships and cases where there's a lot of interaction between the input of a model. This led to the invention of the artificial neural network.

An artificial neural network is a graph composed of several layers of artificial neurons. It's inspired by how the structure and function of the biological brain found in humans and animals.

To understand the power of deep learning and how to use CNTK to build neural networks, we need to look at how a neural network works and how it is trained to detect patterns in samples you feed it.

The neural network architecture

A neural network is made out of different layers. Each layer contains multiple neurons.

A typical neural network is made of several layers of artificial neurons. The first layer in a neural network is called the **input layer**. This is where we feed input into the neural network. The last layer of a neural network is called the **output layer**. This is where the transformed data is coming out of the neural network. The output of a neural network represents the prediction made by the network.

In between the input and output layer of the neural network, you can find one or more hidden layers. The layers in between the input and output are hidden because we don't typically observe the data going through these layers.

Neural networks are mathematical constructs. The data passed through a neural network is encoded as floating-point numbers. This means that everything you want to process with a neural network has to be encoded as vectors of floating-point numbers.

Artificial neurons

The core of a neural network is the artificial neuron. The artificial neuron is the smallest unit in a neural network that we can train to recognize patterns in data. Each artificial neuron inside the neural network has one or more input. Each of the vector input gets a weight:

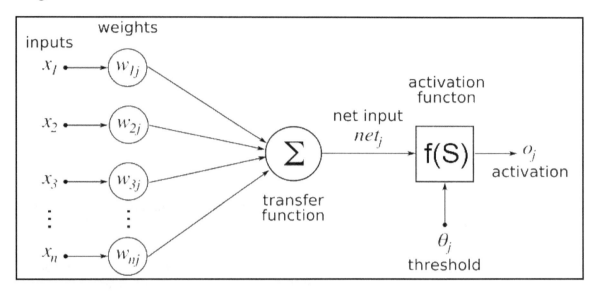

The image is adapted from: https://commons.wikimedia.org/wiki/File:Artificial_neural_network.png

The artificial neuron inside a neural network works in much the same way, but doesn't use chemical signals. Each artificial neuron inside the neural network has one or more inputs. Each of the vector inputs gets a weight.

The numbers provided for each input of the neuron gets multiplied by this weight. The output of this multiplication is then added up to produce a total activation value for the neuron.

This activation signal is then passed through an `activation` function. The `activation` function performs a non-linear transformation on this signal. For example: it uses a `rectified linear` function to process the input signal:

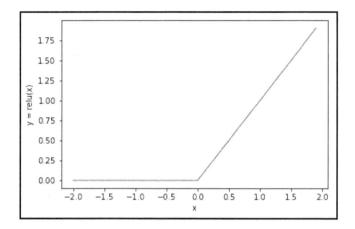

The `rectified linear` function will convert negative activation signals to zero but performs an identity (pass-through) transformation on the signal when it is a positive number.

One other popular activation function is the `sigmoid` function. It behaves slightly different than the `rectified linear` function in that it transforms negative values to 0 and positive values to 1. There is, however, a slope in the activation between -0.5 and +0.5, where the signal is transformed in a linear fashion.

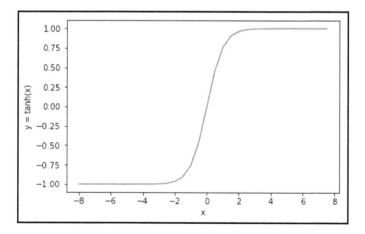

Activation functions in artificial neurons play an important role in the neural network. It's because of these non-linear transformation functions that the neural network is capable of working with non-linear relationships in the data.

Predicting output with a neural network

By combining layers of neurons together we create a stacked function that has non-linear transformations and trainable weights so it can learn to recognize complex relationships. To visualize this, let's transform the neural network from previous sections into a mathematical formula. First, let's take a look at the formula for a single layer:

$$y = f(w * X + b)$$

The X variable is a vector that represents the input for the layer in the neural network. The w parameter represents a vector of weights for each of the elements in the input vector, X. In many neural network implementations, an additional term, b, is added, this is called the **bias** and basically increases or decreases the overall level of input required to activate the neuron. Finally, there's a function, f, which is the `activation` function for the layer.

Now that you've seen the formula for a single layer, let's put together additional layers to create the formula for the neural network:

$$z = f(w_2 * f(w_1 * X + b))$$

Notice how the formula has changed. We now have the formula for the first layer wrapped in another `layer` function. This wrapping or stacking of functions continues when we add more layers to the neural network. Each layer introduces more parameters that need to be optimized to train the neural network. It also allows the neural network to learn more complex relationships from the data we feed into it.

To make a prediction with a neural network, we need to fill all of the parameters in the neural network. Let's assume we know those because we trained it before. What's left is the input value for the neural network.

The input is a vector of floating-point numbers that is a representation of the input of our neural network. The output is a vector that forms a representation of the predicted output of the neural network.

Optimizing a neural network

We've talked about making predictions with neural networks. We haven't yet talked about how to optimize the parameters in a neural network. Let's go over each of the components in a neural network and explore how they work together when we train it:

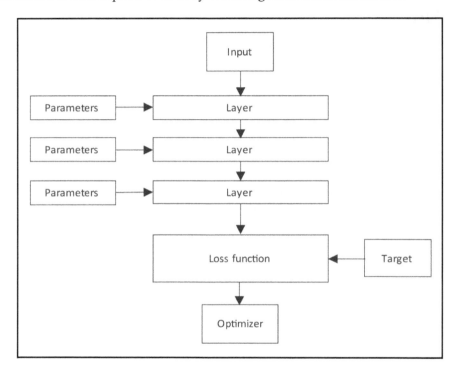

A neural network has several layers that are connected together. Each layer will have a set of trainable parameters that we want to optimize. Optimizing a neural network is done using a technique called backpropagation. We aim to minimize the output of a loss function by gradually optimizing the values for the *w1*, *w2*, and *w3* parameters in the preceding diagram.

The `loss` function for a neural network can take many shapes. Typically, we choose a function that expresses the difference between the expected output, *Y*, and the real output produced by the neural network. For example: we could use the following `loss` function:

$$C = \sum_{i=1}^{n} (Y_i - \hat{Y}_i)^2$$

Firstly, the neural network is initialized with . We can do this with random values for all of the parameters in the model.

After we initialize the neural network, we feed data into the neural network to make a prediction. We then feed the prediction together with the expected output into a `loss` function to measure how close the model is to what we expect it to be.

The feedback from the `loss` function is used to feed an optimizer. The optimizer uses a technique called gradient descent to find out how to optimize each of the parameters.

Gradient descent is a key ingredient of neural network optimization and works because of an interesting property of the `loss` function. When you visualize the output of the `loss` function for one set of input with different values for the parameters in the neural network, you end up with a plot that looks similar to this:

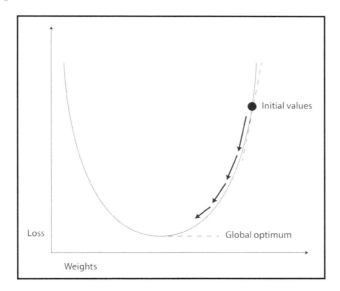

At the beginning of the backpropagation process, we start somewhere on one of the slopes in this mountain landscape. Our aim is to walk down the mountain toward a point where the values for the parameters are at their best. This is the point where the output of the `loss` function is minimized as much as possible.

For us to find the way down the mountain slope, we need to find a function that expresses the slope at the current spot on the mountain slope. We do this by creating a derived function from the `loss` function. This derived function gives us the gradients for the parameters in the model.

When we perform one pass of the backpropagation process, we take one step down the mountain using the gradients for the parameters. We can add the gradients to the parameters to do this. But this is a dangerous way of following the slope down the mountain. Because if we move too fast, we might miss the optimum spot. Therefore, all neural network optimizers have a setting called the learning rate. The learning rate controls the rate of descent.

Because we can only take small steps in the gradient-descent algorithm, we need to repeat this process many times to reach the optimum values for the neural network parameters.

What is CNTK?

Building a neural network from scratch is a big undertaking—something I would not advise anyone to start with unless you're looking for a programming challenge. There are some great libraries that can help you build neural networks without the need to fully understand the mathematical formulas.

Microsoft Cognitive Toolkit (**CNTK**) is an open source library that contains all the basic building blocks to build a neural network.

CNTK is implemented using C++ and Python, but it is also available in C# and Java. Training can only be done in C++ or Python, but you can easily load your models in C# or Java for making predictions after you've trained your neural network.

There is also a variant of CNTK that uses a proprietary language called BrainScript. But for the purpose of this book, we'll only look at Python for the basic features of the framework. Later on, in `Chapter 7`, *Deploying Models to Production*, we'll discuss how to use C# or Java to load and use a trained model.

Features of CNTK

CNTK is a library that has both a low-level and high-level API for building neural networks. The low-level API is meant for scientists looking to build the next generation of neural network components, while the high-level API is meant for building production-quality neural networks.

On top of these basic building blocks, CNTK features a set of components that will make it easier to feed data into your neural network. It also contains various components to monitor and debug neural networks.

Finally, CNTK features a C# and Java API. You can use both of these languages to load trained models and make predictions from within your web application, microservices, or even Windows Store apps. In addition, you can use C# to train models should you want to do this.

Although it is possible to work with CNTK from Java and C#, it is important to know that at this point not all features in the Python version of CNTK are available to the C# and Java APIs. For example: models trained for object detection in Python do not work in C# with version 2.6 of CNTK.

A high-speed low-level API

At the core of CNTK, you'll find a low-level API that contains a set of mathematical operators to build neural network components. The low-level API also includes the automatic differentiation needed to optimize the parameters in your neural network.

Microsoft built the components with high performance in mind. For example: it included specific code to train neural networks on graphics cards. Graphics cards contain specialized processors, called GPUs, that are capable of processing large volumes of vector and matrix math at very high speeds. You can typically speed up the training process of a neural network by at least a factor 10.

Basic building blocks for quickly creating neural networks

When you want to build a neural network for production use, you typically use the high-level API. The high-level API contains all kinds of different building blocks of a neural network.

For example: there's a basic dense layer to build the most basic kind of neural network. But you will also find more advanced layer types in the high-level API, such as the layer types needed to process images or time series data.

The high-level API also contains different optimizers to train neural networks, so you don't have to manually build a gradient-descent optimizer. In CNTK, the optimization process is implemented using learners and trainers, where the learner defines which kind of gradient-descent algorithm to use while the trainer defines how to implement the basics of backpropagation.

In Chapter 2, *Building Neural Networks with CNTK*, we'll explore how to use the high-level API to build and train a neural network. In Chapter 5, *Working with Images*, and Chapter 6, *Working with Time Series Data,* you'll learn how to use some of the more advanced layer types to process images and time series data with CNTK.

Measuring model performance

Once you've built a neural network, you want to make sure that it works correctly. CNTK offers a number of components to measure the performance of neural networks.

You will often find yourself looking for ways to monitor how well the training process for your model is doing. CNTK includes components that will generate log data from your model and the associated optimizer, which you can use to monitor the training process.

Loading and processing large datasets

When you use deep learning, you often need a large dataset to train neural networks. It is not uncommon to use gigabytes of data to train your model. Included with CNTK is a set of components that allow you to feed data into the neural network for training.

Microsoft did its best to build specialized readers that will load data into memory in batches so you don't need a terabyte of RAM to train your network. We'll talk about these readers in greater depth in Chapter 3, *Getting Data into Your Neural Network*.

Using models from C# and Java

The main CNTK library is built in Python on top of a C++ core. You can use both C++ and Python to train models. When you want to use your models in production, you have a lot more choice. You can use your trained model from C++ or Python, but most developers will want to use Java or C#. Python is much slower than these languages when it comes to runtime performance. Also, C# and Java are more widely used in corporate environments.

You can download the C# and Java version of CNTK as a separate library from NuGet or Maven central. In `Chapter 7`, *Deploying Models to Production*, we'll discuss how to use CNTK from these languages to host a trained model inside a microservice environment.

Installing CNTK

Now that we've seen how neural networks work and what CNTK is, let's take a look at how to install it on your computer. CNTK is supported on both Windows and Linux, so we'll walk through each of them.

Installing on Windows

We will be using the Anaconda version of Python on Windows to run CNTK. Anaconda is a redistribution of Python that includes additional packages, such as `SciPy` and `scikit-learn`, which are used by CNTK to perform various calculations.

Installing Anaconda

You can download Anaconda from the public website: `https://www.anaconda.com/download/`.

After you've downloaded the setup files, start the installation and follow the instructions to install Anaconda on your computer. You can find the installation instructions at `https://docs.anaconda.com/anaconda/install/`.

Anaconda will install a number of utilities on your computer. It will install a new command prompt that will automatically include all the Anaconda executables in your PATH variable. You can quickly manage your Python environment from this command prompt, install packages and, of course, run Python scripts.

Optionally, you can install Visual Studio Code with your Anaconda installation. Visual Studio Code is a code editor similar to Sublime and Atom and contains a large number of plugins that make it easier to write program code in different programming languages, such as Python.

CNTK 2.6 supports Python 3.6 only, which means that not all distributions of Anaconda will work correctly. You can get an older version of Anaconda through the Anaconda archives at `https://repo.continuum.io/archive/`. Alternatively, you can downgrade the Python version in your Anaconda installation if you haven't got a version with Python 3.6 included. To install Python 3.6 in your Anaconda environment, open a new Anaconda prompt and execute the following command:

```
conda install python=3.6
```

Upgrading pip

Anaconda comes with a slightly outdated version of the python package manager, `pip`. This can cause problems when we try to install the CNTK package. So, before we install the CNTK package, let's upgrade the `pip` executable.

To upgrade the `pip` executable, open the Anaconda prompt and execute the following command:

```
python -m pip install --upgrade pip
```

This will remove the old `pip` executable and install a new version in its place.

Installing CNTK

There's a number of ways to get the CNTK package on your computer. The most common way is to install the package through the `pip` executable:

```
pip install cntk
```

This will download the CNTK package from the package manager website and install it on your machine. `pip` will automatically check for missing dependencies and install those as well.

There are several alternative methods to install CNTK on your machine. The website has a neat set of documentation that explains the other installation methods in great detail: `https://docs.microsoft.com/en-us/cognitive-toolkit/Setup-CNTK-on-your-machine`.

Installing on Linux

Installing CNTK on Linux is slightly different than installing it on Windows. Just as on Windows, we will use Anaconda to run the CNTK package. But instead of a graphical installer for Anaconda, there's a terminal-based installer on Linux. The installer will work on most Linux distributions. We limited the description to Ubuntu, a widely-used Linux distribution.

Installing Anaconda

Before we can install Anaconda, we need to make sure that the system is fully up to date. To check this, execute the following two commands inside a terminal:

```
sudo apt update
sudo apt upgrade
```

Automatically Programmed Tool (APT) is used to install all sorts of packages inside Ubuntu. In the code sample, we first ask apt to update the references to the various package repositories. We then ask it to install the latest updates.

After the computer is updated, we can start the installation of Anaconda. First, navigate to https://www.anaconda.com/download/ to get the URL for the latest Anaconda installation files. You can right-click on the download link and copy the URL to your clipboard.

Now open up a terminal window and execute the following command:

```
wget -O anaconda-installer.sh url
```

Make sure to replace the url placeholder with the URL you copied from the Anaconda website. Press *Enter* to execute the command.

Once the installation file is download, you can install Anaconda by running the following command:

```
sh ./anaconda-installer.sh
```

This will start the installer. Follow the instructions on the screen to install Anaconda on your computer. By default, Anaconda gets installed in a folder called anaconda3 inside your home directory.

As is the case with the Windows version of CNTK 2.6, it only supports Python 3.6. You can either get an older distribution of Anaconda through their archives at `https://repo.continuum.io/archive/`, or downgrade your Python version by executing the following command in your terminal:

```
conda install python=3.6
```

Upgrading pip to the latest version

Once we have Anaconda installed, we need to upgrade `pip` to the latest version. `pip` is used to install packages inside Python. It is the tool we're going to use to install CNTK:

```
python -m pip install --upgrade pip
```

Installing the CNTK package

The final step in the installation process is to install CNTK. This is done through `pip` using the following command:

```
pip install cntk
```

Should you want to, you can also install CNTK by downloading a wheel file directly or using an installer with Anaconda included. You can find more information on alternative installation methods for CNTK at `https://docs.microsoft.com/en-us/cognitive-toolkit/Setup-CNTK-on-your-machine`.

Using your GPU with CNTK

We looked at how to install the basic version of CNTK for use with your CPU. While the `CNTK` package is fast, it will run quicker on a GPU. But not all machines support this setup, and that's why I put the description of how to use your GPU into a separate section.

Before you attempt to install CNTK for use with a GPU, make sure you have a supported graphics card. Currently, CNTK supports the NVIDIA graphics card with at least CUDA 3.0 support. CUDA is the programming API from NVIDIA that allows developers to run non-graphical programs on their graphics cards. You can check whether your graphics card supports CUDA on this website: `https://developer.nvidia.com/cuda-gpus`.

Enabling GPU usage on Windows

To use your graphics card with CNTK on Windows, you need to have the latest GeForce or Quadro drivers for your graphics card (depending on which one you have). Aside from the latest drivers, you need to install the CUDA toolkit Version 9.0 for Windows.

You can download the CUDA toolkit from the NVIDIA website: `https://developer.nvidia.com/cuda-90-download-archive?target_os=Windowstarget_arch=x86_64`. Once downloaded, run the installer and follow the instructions on the screen.

CNTK uses a layer on top of CUDA, called cuDNN, for neural-network-specific primitives. You can download the cuDNN binaries from the NVIDIA website at `https://developer.nvidia.com/rdp/form/cudnn-download-survey`. In contrast to the CUDA toolkit, you need to register an account to the website before you can download the cuDNN binaries.

Not all cuDNN binaries work with every version of CUDA. The website mentions which version of cuDNN is compatible with which version of the CUDA toolkit. For CUDA 9.0, you need to download cuDNN 7.4.1.

Once you have downloaded the cuDNN binaries, extract the zip file into the root folder of your CUDA toolkit installation. Typically, the CUDA toolkit is located at `C:\program files\NVIDIA GPU Computing Toolkit\CUDA\v9.0`.

The final step to enable GPU usage inside CNTK is to install the `CNTK-GPU` package. Open the Anaconda prompt in Windows and execute the following command:

```
pip install cntk-gpu
```

Enabling GPU usage on Linux

Using your graphics card with CNTK on Linux requires that you run the proprietary drivers for NVIDIA. When you install the CUDA toolkit on your Linux machine, you get asked to install the latest drivers for your graphics card automatically. While you are not required to install the drivers through the CUDA toolkit installer, we strongly recommend you do, as the drivers will match the binaries of the CUDA toolkit. This reduces the risk of a failing installation or other errors later on.

You can download the CUDA toolkit from the NVIDIA website: `https://developer.nvidia.com/cuda-90-download-archive?target_os=Linuxtarget_arch=x86_64target_distro=Ubuntutarget_version=1604target_type=runfilelocal`.

Please make sure you select the appropriate Linux distribution and version. The link automatically selects Ubuntu 16.04 and uses a local runfile.

Once you've downloaded the binaries to disk, you can run the installer by opening a terminal and executing the following command:

```
sh cuda_9.0.176_384.81_linux-run
```

Follow the onscreen instructions to install the CUDA toolkit on your machine.

Once you have the CUDA toolkit installed, you need to modify your Bash profile script. Open the $HOME/.bashrc file in your favorite text editor and include the following lines at the end of the script:

```
export PATH=/usr/local/cuda-9.0/bin${PATH:+:${PATH}}
export LD_LIBRARY_PATH=/usr/local/cuda-9.0/lib64\
        ${LD_LIBRARY_PATH:+:${LD_LIBRARY_PATH}}
```

The first line includes the CUDA binaries in the PATH variable so CNTK can access them. The second line in the script includes the CNTK libraries in your library PATH so CNTK can load them when needed.

Save the changes to the file and close the editor. Please make sure you restart your terminal window to ensure that the new settings are loaded.

The final step is to download and install the cuDNN binaries. CNTK uses a layer on top of CUDA, called cuDNN, for neural-network-specific primitives. You can download the cuDNN binaries from the NVIDIA website here: https://developer.nvidia.com/rdp/form/cudnn-download-survey. In contrast to the CUDA toolkit, you need to register an account on the website before you can download the cuDNN binaries.

Not all cuDNN binaries work with every version of CUDA. The website mentions which version of cuDNN is compatible with which version of the CUDA toolkit. For CUDA 9.0, you need to download cuDNN 7.4.1. Download the version for Linux and extract it to the /usr/local/cuda-9.0 folder using the following command:

```
tar xvzf -C /usr/local/cuda-9.0/ cudnn-9.0-linux-x64-v7.4.1.5.tgz
```

The filename may differ slightly; change the path to the filename as needed.

Summary

In this chapter, we learned about deep learning and its relationship to machine learning and AI. We looked at the basic concepts behind deep learning and how to train a neural network using gradient descent. We then talked about CNTK, what it is, and what features the library offers to build deep learning models. We finally spent some time discussing how to install CNTK on Windows and Linux and how to use your GPU should you want to.

In the next chapter, we will learn how to build basic neural networks with CNTK so we get a better understanding of how the concepts in this chapter work in code. We will also discuss the different ways we can use various components in our deep learning model for different scenarios.

Building Neural Networks with

2

CNTK

In the previous chapter, we talked about what deep learning is, and how neural networks work on a conceptual level. Finally, we talked about CNTK, and how to get it installed on your machine. In this chapter, we will build our first neural network with CNTK and train it.

We will look at building a neural network using the different functions and classes from the CNTK library. We will do this with a basic classification problem.

Once we have a neural network for our classification problem, we will train it with sample data obtained from an open dataset. After our neural network is trained, we will look at how to use it to make predictions.

At the end of this chapter, we will spend some time talking about ways to improve your model once you've trained it.

In this chapter, we will cover the following topics:

- Basic neural network concepts in CNTK
- Building your first neural network
- Training the neural network
- Making predictions with a neural network
- Improving the model

Technical requirements

In this chapter, we will work on a sample model, built using Python in a Jupyter notebook. Jupyter is an open source technology that allows you to create interactive web pages that contain sections of Python code, Markdown, and HTML. It makes it much easier to document your code and assumptions you made while building your deep learning model.

If you've installed Anaconda using the steps defined in Chapter 1, *Getting Started with CNTK*, you already have Jupyter installed on your machine. Should you not have Anaconda yet, you can download it from: https://anacondacloud.com/download.

You can get the sample code for this chapter from: https://github.com/PacktPublishing/Deep-Learning-with-Microsoft-Cognitive-Toolkit-Quick-Start-Guide/tree/master/ch2. To run the sample code, run the following commands inside a Terminal in the directory where you downloaded the sample code:

```
cd ch2
jupyter notebook
```

Look for the Train your first model.ipynb notebook, and click it to open up the sample code. You can execute all the code in one step by choosing **Cell | Run All**. This will execute all the steps in the notebook.

Check out the following video to see the code in action:

http://bit.ly/2YoyNKY

Basic neural network concepts in CNTK

In the previous chapter, we looked at the basic concepts of a neural network. Let's map the concepts we've learned to components in the CNTK library, and discover how you can use these concepts to build your own model.

Building neural networks using layer functions

Neural networks are made using several layers of neurons. In CNTK, we can model the layers of a neural network using layer functions defined in the layers module. A `layer` function in CNTK looks like a regular function. For example, you can create the most basic layer type, `Dense`, with one line of code:

```
from cntk.layers import Dense
from cntk import input_variable

features = input_variable(100)
layer = Dense(50)(features)
```

To Create the most basic layer type following the given steps:

1. First, import the `Dense` layer function from the layers package
2. Next, import the `input_variable` function from the `cntk` root package
3. Create a new input variable with the name features using the `input_variable` function and give it a size of `100`
4. Create a new layer using the `Dense` function providing it with the number of neurons you want
5. Invoke the configured `Dense` layer function providing the features variable to connect the `Dense` layer to the input

Working with layers in CNTK has a distinct functional programming feel to it. When we look at the previous chapter, we can understand why CNTK has gone down this route. Ultimately, every layer in a neural network is a mathematical function. All the layer functions in CNTK produce a mathematical function with a set of predefined parameters. Invoke the function again, and you bind the last missing parameter, the input, to the layer.

You will typically build neural networks with this style of programming when you want to create a neural network with a complex architecture. But, for most starting developers, the functional style feels unfamiliar. CNTK provides an easier API for when you want to build a basic neural network through the `Sequential` layer function.

You can use the `Sequential` layer function to chain several layers together, without having to use the functional programming style, as follows:

```
from cntk.layers import Sequential, Dense
from cntk import input_variable

features = input_variable(7)
```

```
network = Sequential([
   Dense(64),
   Dense(32),
   Dense(3)
]) (features)
```

To do so, follow the given steps:

1. First, import the layer functions you want to use from the `layers` package
2. Import the the `input_variable` function to create an input variable used to feed data into the neural network
3. Create a new input variable to feed data into the neural network
4. Create a new sequential layer block by invoking the `Sequential` function
5. Provide the list of layers that you want to chain together to the `Sequential` function
6. Invoke the configured `Sequential` function object providing the features input variable to complete the network structure

By combining the `Sequential` function and other layer functions you can create any neural network structure. In the next section, we'll take a look at how to customize layers with settings to configure things like the `activation` function.

Customizing layer settings

CNTK provides a pretty good set of defaults for building neural networks. But you'll find yourself experimenting with those settings a lot. The behavior and performance of the neural network will be different based on the `activation` function and other settings you choose. Because of this, it is good to understand what you can configure.

Each layer has its own unique configuration options, some of which you will use a lot, and others you will use less. When we look at the `Dense` layer, there are a few important settings that you want to define:

- `shape`: The output shape of the layer
- `activation`: The `activation` function for the layer
- `init`: The `initialization` function of the layer

The output shape of a layer determines the number of neurons in that layer. Each neuron needs to have an `activation` function defined so it can transform the input data. Finally, we need a function that will initialize the parameters of the layer when we start training the neural network. The output shape is the first parameter in each `layer` function. The `activation` and `init` arguments are supplied as keyword arguments. These parameters have default values for them, so you can omit them should you not need a custom setting. The next sample demonstrates how to configure a `Dense` layer with a custom `initializer` and `activation` function:

```
from cntk.layers import Dense
from cntk.ops import sigmoid
from cntk.initializer import glorot_uniform

layer = Dense(128, activation=sigmoid, init=glorot_uniform)
```

To configure a Dense layer follow the given steps:

1. First, import the `Dense` layer from the `layers` package
2. Next, import the `sigmoid` operator from the `ops` package so we can use it to configure as an `activation` function
3. Then import the `glorot_uniform` initializer from the `initializer` package
4. Finally, create a new layer using the `Dense` layer providing the number of neurons as the first argument and provide the `sigmoid` operator as the `activation` function and the `glorot_uniform` function as the `init` function for the layer

There are several `activation` functions to choose from; for example, you can use **Rectified Linear Unit (ReLU)**, or `sigmoid`, as an `activation` function. All `activation` functions can be found in the `cntk.ops` package.

Each `activation` function will have a different effect on the performance of your neural network. We will go into more detail regarding `activation` functions when we build a neural network later in this chapter.

Initializers determine how the parameters in the layer are initialized when we start training our neural network. You can choose from various initializers in CNTK. `Normal`, `uniform`, and `glorot_uniform` are some of the more widely used initializers in the `cntk.initializer` package. We will get into more detail about which initializer to use when we start to solve our first deep learning problem.

Whatever initializer function you're using from CNTK, it's important to realize that they use random number generators to generate the initial values for the parameters in the layer. This is an important technique, because it allows the neural network to learn the right parameters effectively. All initializer functions in CNTK support an extra seed setting. When you set this parameter to a fixed value, you will get the same initial values every time you train your neural network. This can be useful when you're trying to reproduce a problem, or are experimenting with different settings.

When you are building a neural network, you typically have to specify the same set of settings for several layers in your neural network. This can become problematic when you are experimenting with your model. To solve this, CNTK includes a `utility` function called `default_options`:

```
from cntk import default_options
from cntk.layers import Dense, Sequential
from cntk.ops import sigmoid

with default_options(activation=sigmoid):
  network = Sequential([
    Dense(1024),
    Dense(512),
    Dense(256)
  ])
```

By using the `default_options` function, we've configured the `sigmoid` activation function for all three layers, with just one line of code. The `default_options` function accepts a standard set of settings that get applied to all layers in the scope of this function. Using the `default_options` function makes configuring the same options for a set of layers much more comfortable. You can configure quite a lot of settings this way; for example, with the following functions:

- `activation`: The `activation` function to use
- `init`: The `initialization` function for the layers
- `bias`: Whether the layers should have a `bias` term included
- `init_bias`: The `initialization` function for the bias term

Using learners and trainers to optimize the parameters in a neural network

In the previous sections we've seen how to create the structure for a neural network and how to configure various settings. Now let's look at how to use `learners` and `trainers` to optimize the parameters of a neural network. In CNTK, a neural network is trained using a combination of two components. The first component is the `trainer` component, which implements the backpropagation process. The second component is the `learner`. It is responsible for performing the gradient descent algorithm that we've seen in `Chapter 1`, *Getting Started with CNTK*.

The `trainer` passes the data through the neural network to obtain a prediction. It then uses the `learner` to obtain the new values for the parameters in the neural network. It then applies these new values, and repeats the process. This goes on until an exit criterion is met. The training process is stopped when a configured number of iterations is reached. This can be enhanced using custom callbacks.

We've discussed a very basic form of gradient descent in `Chapter 1`, *Getting Started with CNTK*. But, in reality, there are many variations on this basic algorithm. The basic gradient descent doesn't work very well for complex cases. Often, it gets stuck in a local optimum (a bump in the hillside, if you will), so it doesn't reach a globally optimal value for the parameters in the neural network. Other algorithms, such as **Stochastic Gradient Descent (SGD)** with momentum, account for local optima, and use concepts such as momentum to get past bumps in the slope of the loss curve.

Here are few interesting `learners` that are included in the CNTK library:

- **SGD**: The basic stochastic gradient descent, without any extras
- **MomentumSGD**: Applies momentum to overcome local optima
- **RMSProp**: Uses decaying learning rates to control the rate of descent
- **Adam**: Uses decaying momentum to decrease the rate of descent over time
- **Adagrad**: Uses different learning rates for frequently, and infrequently, occurring features

It's important to know that you can choose different `learners`, depending on the problem you want to solve. We will learn more about choosing the right optimizer when we start to solve our first machine learning problem with a neural network.

Loss functions

In order for the `trainer` and `learner` to be able to optimize the parameters of the neural network, we need to define a function that measures the loss in the neural network. The `loss` function calculates how big the difference is between the predicted output of the neural network, and the expected output that we know beforehand.

CNTK contains a number of `loss` functions in the `cntk.losses` module. Each `loss` function has its own use and specific characteristics. For example, when you want to measure the loss in a model that predicts a continuous value, you're going to need the `squared_error` loss function. It measures the distance between the predicted value generated by the model, and the real value that you provided when training the model.

For classification models, you will need a different set of `loss` functions. The `binary_cross_entropy` loss function can be used to measure the loss in a model that is used for binary classification jobs, such as a fraud detection model. The `cross_entropy_with_softmax` loss function is more suitable for classification models that predict multiple classes.

Model metrics

Combining a `learner` and `loss` function with a `trainer` allows us to optimize the parameters in the neural network. This should produce a good model, but in order to know that for sure we need metrics to measure model performance. A metric is a single value that tells us, for example, what percentage of samples was predicted correctly.

Because the `loss` function measures the difference between the actual value and the predicted value, you might think that it's a good measure of how well our model is doing. Depending on the model, it may provide some value, but often you will need to use a separate `metric` function to measure your model's performance in a meaningful way.

CNTK offers a number of different `metric` functions in the `cntk.metrics` package. For example, if you want to measure the performance of a classification model, you can use the `classification_error` function. This is used to measure the percentage of samples that were predicted correctly.

The `classification_error` function is just one example of a metric. One other important `metric` function is the `ndcg_at_1` metric. If you're working with a ranking model, then you are interested in how closely your model ranked the samples according to a predefined ranking. This is what the `ndcg_at_1` metric gives you.

Building your first neural network

Now that we've learned what concepts CNTK offers to build a neural network, we can start to apply these concepts to a real machine learning problem. In this section, we'll explore how to use a neural network to classify species of iris flowers.

This is not a typical task where you want to use a neural network. But, as you will soon discover, the dataset is simple enough to get a good grasp of the process of building a deep learning model. Yet it contains enough data to ensure that the model works reasonably well.

The iris dataset describes the physical properties of different varieties of iris flowers:

- Sepal length in cm
- Sepal width in cm
- Petal length in cm
- Petal width in cm
- Class (iris setosa, iris versicolor, iris virginica)

 The code for this chapter includes the iris dataset, on which you need to train the deep learning model. If you're interested, you can find the original files online at: http://archive.ics.uci.edu/ml/datasets/Iris. It is also included with the sample code for this chapter.

We are going to build a deep learning model that is going to classify a flower based on the physical properties of sepal width and length, and petal width and length. We can predict three different classes as output for the model.

We have a total of 150 different samples to train on, which should be enough to get reasonable performance when we try to use the model to classify a flower.

Building the network structure

First, we need to determine what architecture to use for our neural network. We will be building a regular neural network, which is often called a feedforward neural network.

We need to define the number of neurons on the input and output layers first. Then, we need to define the shape of the hidden layer in our neural network. Because the task that we're solving is a simple one, we don't need more than one layer.

When we look at our dataset, we can see it has four features and one label. Because we have four features, we need to make sure our neural network has an input layer with four neurons.

Next, we need to define the output layer for our neural network. For this, we look at the number of classes that we need to be able to predict with our model. In our case, we have three different species of flowers to choose from, so we need three neurons in the output layer.

First, we import the necessary components from the CNTK library, which are our layer types, `activation` functions, and a function that allows us to define an input variable for our network:

```
from cntk import default_options, input_variable
from cntk.layers import Dense, Sequential
from cntk.ops import log_softmax, relu
```

We then create our model using the `Sequential` function, and feed it the layers that we want. We create two distinct layers in our network—first, one with four neurons, and then, another one with three neurons:

```
model = Sequential([
    Dense(4, activation=relu),
    Dense(3, activation=log_softmax)
])
```

Finally, we bind the network to the input variable, which will compile the neural network so it has an input layer with four neurons, and an output layer with three neurons, as follows:

```
features = input_variable(4)
z = model(features)
```

Now, let's go back to our layer structure. Notice that we didn't model an input layer when we invoked the `Sequential` layer function. This is because the `input_variable` we created in our code is the input layer for the neural network.

The first layer in the sequential call is the hidden layer in the network. As a general rule of thumb, you want hidden layers that are no bigger than two times the number of neurons in the previous layer.

You will want to experiment with this setup in order to get the best results. Picking the right numbers of layers and neurons in your neural network requires some experience and experimentation. There are no hard rules that determine how many hidden layers you should include.

Choosing an activation function

In the previous section, we chose the `sigmoid` activation function for our neural network. Choosing the right activation makes a big difference to how well your deep learning model will perform.

You will find a lot of opinions about choosing an `activation` function. That's because there's a lot to choose from, and not enough hard proof for any of the choices made by experts in the field. So, how do you pick one for your neural network?

Choosing an activation function for the output layer

First, we need to define what kind of problem we're solving. This determines the `activation` function for the output layer of your network. For regression problems, you want to use a `linear` activation function on the output layer. For a classification problem, you will want to use `sigmoid` for binary classification, and the `softmax` function for multi-class classification problems.

In the model that we're building, we need to predict one of three classes, which means we need to use the `softmax` activation function on the output layer.

Choosing an activation function for the hidden layers

Now, let's look at the hidden layers. Choosing an `activation` function for the hidden layers in our model is much harder. We will need to run some experiments and monitor the performance to see which `activation` function works best.

For classification problems, like our flower classification model, we need something that gives us probabilistic values. We need this because we need to predict the probability a sample belongs to a specific class. The `sigmoid` function helps us reach this goal. Its output is a probability, measured as a value between 0 and 1.

There are some problems that we have to account for with a `sigmoid` activation function. When you create larger networks, you may run into a problem called the **vanishing gradient**.

Very large input values given to a `sigmoid` function will converge to either zero or one, depending on whether they are negative or positive. This means that, when we work with large input values for our model, we won't see a lot of difference in the output of the `sigmoid` function. A change in an already large input value will result in only a very small change in the output. The gradient that is derived from this by the optimizer during training is also very small. Sometimes, it is so small that your computer will round it to zero, which means the optimizer can't detect which way to go with the values for the parameters. When the optimizer can't calculate gradients because of rounding problems in the CPU, we're dealing with a vanishing gradient problem.

To solve this problem, scientists have come up with a new activation function, `ReLU`. This activation function converts all negative values to zero, and works as a pass-through filter for positive values. It helps solve the vanishing gradient problem, because it doesn't limit the output value.

There are, however, two problems with the `ReLU` function. First, it converts negative input to zero. In some cases, this can lead to a situation where the optimizer sets the weight of some parameters to zero as well. This causes your network to have dead neurons. That, of course, limits what your network can do.

The second problem is that the `ReLU` function suffers from exploding gradients. Because the upper bound of the output of this function isn't limited, it can amplify signals in such a way that the optimizer will calculate gradients that are close to infinity. When you apply this gradient to parameters in your network, your network will start to output NaN values.

Choosing the correct activation function for hidden layers requires some experimentation. Again, there is no hard rule that says which activation function to use. In the example code of this chapter, we choose the `sigmoid` function, after experimenting a bit with the model.

Picking a loss function

When we have the structure for the model, it is time to take a look at how to optimize it. For this, we need a `loss` function to minimize. There are quite a few `loss` functions to choose from.

The right `loss` function depends on what kind of problem you are solving. For example, in a classification model like ours, we need a `loss` function that can measure the difference between a predicted class and an actual class. It needs to do so for three classes. The `categorical cross entropy` function is a good candidate. In CNTK, this `loss` function is implemented as `cross_entropy_with_softmax`:

```
label = input_variable(3)
loss = cross_entropy_with_softmax(z, label)
```

We need to import the `cross_entropy_with_softmax` function from the `cntk.losses` package first. After we've imported the `loss` function, we create a new input variable so we can feed the expected label into the `loss` function. Then we create a new `loss` variable that will hold a reference to the `loss` function. Any `loss` function in CNTK requires the output of the model and an input variable for the expected label.

Recording metrics

With the structure in place and a `loss` function, we have all the ingredients we need to start optimizing our deep learning model. But before we start to look at how to train the model, let's take a look at metrics.

In order for us to see how our network is doing, we need to record some metrics. Since we're building a classification model, we're going to use a `classification_error` metric. This metric produces a number between 0 and 1, which indicates the percentage of samples correctly predicted:

```
error_rate = classification_error(z, label)
```

Let's import `classification_error` from the `cntk.metrics` package. We then create a new `error_rate` variable and bind the `classification_error` function to it. The function needs the output of the network and the expected label as input. We already have those available from defining our model and `loss` function.

Training the neural network

Now that we have all the components for the deep learning defined, let's train it. You can train a model in CNTK using a combination of a `learner` and `trainer`. We're going to need to define those and then feed data through the trainer to train the model. Let's see how that works.

Choosing a learner and setting up training

There are several `learners` to choose from. For our first model, we are going to use the `stochastic gradient descent` learner. Let's configure the `learner` and `trainer` to train the neural network:

```
from cntk.learners import sgd
from cntk.train.trainer import Trainer

learner = sgd(z.parameters, 0.01)

trainer = Trainer(z, (loss, error_rate), [learner])
```

To configure the `learner` and `trainer` to train the neural network, follow the given steps:

1. First, import the `sgd` function from the `learners` package
2. Then, import the `Trainer` from the `trainer` package which is part of the `train` package

3. Now create a `learner` by invoking the `sgd` function providing the parameters of the model and a value for the learning rate
4. Finally, initialize the `trainer` and provide it the network, the combination of the `loss` and `metric` and the `learner`

The learning rate that we provide to the `sgd` function controls the speed of optimization and should be a small number somewhere in the area of 0.1 to 0.001.

Note that every `learner` has its own parameters, so be sure to check the documentation to find out what parameters you need to configure when using a specific `learner` from the `cntk.learners` package.

Feeding data into the trainer to optimize the neural network

We spent quite a bit of time defining our model, configuring the `loss`, `metrics`, and, finally, the `learner`. Now it is time to train it on our dataset. Before we can train our model, however, we need to load the dataset.

The dataset in the example code is stored as a CSV file. In order to load this dataset, we need to use a data wrangling package such as `pandas`. This package is included by default in your Anaconda installation. The following sample demonstrates how to use `pandas` to load the dataset into memory:

```
import pandas as pd

df_source = pd.read_csv('iris.csv',
    names=['sepal_length', 'sepal_width','petal_length','petal_width',
'species'],
    index_col=False)
```

To load the dataset into memory using `pandas` follow the given steps:

1. First, import the `pandas` package under the alias `pd`
2. Then, invoke the `read_csv` function to load the `iris.csv` file from disk

Because the CSV file doesn't include column headers, we need to define them ourselves. It will make it easier to refer to specific columns later on.

Normally, `pandas` will use the first column in the input file as the index of the dataset. The index will serve as a key by which you can identify records. We don't have an index in our dataset, so we disable its use through the `index_col` keyword argument.

After we have loaded the dataset, let's split it into a set of features and a label:

```
X = df_source.iloc[:, :4].values
y = df_source['species'].values
```

To split the dataset into a set of features and label, follow the given steps:

1. First, use the `iloc` function to select all rows and the first four columns from the dataset
2. Next, select the species column from the dataset and use the values property to access the underlying `numpy` array

Our model requires numeric input values. But the species column is a string value, indicating the type of flower. We can fix this by encoding the species column to a numeric vector representation. The vector representation we're creating matches the number of output neurons of the neural network. Each element in the vector represents a species of flowers as follows:

```
label_mapping = {
    'Iris-setosa': 0,
    'Iris-versicolor': 1,
```

```
    'Iris-virginica': 2
}
```

To create one-hot vector representations for the species, we will use a small `utility` function:

```
def one_hot(index, length):
    result = np.zeros(length)
    result[index] = 1
    return result
```

The `one_hot` function performs the following steps:

1. First, initialize a new array filled with zeros with the required `length`
2. Next, select the element at the specified `index` and set it to `1`

Now that we have a dictionary mapping the species to the index, and a way to create one-hot vectors, we can turn the string values into their vector representation using one additional line of code:

```
y = np.array([one_hot(label_mapping[v], 3) for v in y])
```

Follow the given steps:

1. First, create a list expression to iterate over all elements in the array
2. For each value in the array perform a look up in the `label_mapping` dictionary
3. Next, take this converted numeric value and apply the `one_hot` function to convert it to a one-hot encoded vector
4. Finally, take the converted list and turn it into a `numpy` array

When you are training a deep learning model, or any machine learning model for that matter, you need to keep in mind that the computer will try to remember all the samples that you've used for training the model. At the same time, it will try to learn general rules. When the model remembers samples, but isn't able to deduce rules from the training samples, it is overfitting on your dataset.

To detect overfitting, you want to keep a small portion of your dataset separate from the training set. The training set is then used to train the model, while the test set is used to measure the performance of the model.

We can split our dataset into training and test sets using a `utility` function from the `scikit-learn` package:

```
from sklearn.model_selection import train_test_split

X_train, X_test, y_train, y_test = train_test_split(X,y, test_size=0.2,
stratify=y)
```

Follow the given steps:

1. First, import the `train_test_split` function from the `model_selection` module in the `sklearn` package
2. Then, invoke the `train_test_split` function with the features X and the labels y
3. Specify a `test_size` of `0.2` to set aside 20% of the data
4. Use the `stratify` keyword argument with the values from the labels array y so that we get an equal amount of samples in the training and test set for each of the species in the dataset

If you don't use the `stratify` argument, you end up with a dataset that might not contain any samples for one class, while it has too many of another class. The model then doesn't learn how to classify the class that is missing in the training set, while it overfits on the other class, which has too many samples available.

Now that we have a training set and validation set, let's see how to feed them to our model to train it:

```
trainer.train_minibatch({ features: X_train, label: y_train })
```

To train the model, invoke the `train_minibatch` method on the `trainer` and give it a dictionary that maps the input data to the input variables that you used to define the neural network and its associated `loss` function.

We're using the `train_minibatch` method as a convenient way to feed data into the trainer. In the next chapter, we'll discuss other ways to feed data. We'll also look at what the `train_minibatch` method does in greater detail.

Note that you will have to call `train_minibatch` a number of times to get the network decently trained. So we'll have to write a short loop around this method call:

```
for _epoch in range(10):
    trainer.train_minibatch({ features: X_train, label: y_train })

    print('Loss: {}, Acc: {}'.format(
```

```
trainer.previous_minibatch_loss_average,
trainer.previous_minibatch_evaluation_average))
```

Follow the given steps:

1. First, create a new loop using the `for` statement and give it a range of `10`
2. Within the loop invoke the `train_minibatch` method with a mapping between the input variables and the associated data
3. Finally, print the `previous_minibatch_loss_average` and `previous_minibatch_evaluation_average` to monitor the training progress.

When you invoke the `train_minibatch` method, the `trainer` will update the output of the `loss` function and the value for the `metric` function that we provided to the `trainer` and store it in the `previous_minibatch_evaluation_average`.

Each time the loop completes, and we've run the whole dataset through the `trainer`, we've completed one epoch of training. As we have seen in the previous chapter, it is normal to run several epochs before a model works well enough. As an added bonus, we're also printing the progress of our `trainer` after each epoch.

Checking the performance of the neural network

Every time we pass data through the trainer to optimize our model, it measures the performance of the model through the metric that we configured for the trainer. The model performance measured during training is on the training set. It is useful to measure the accuracy on the training set, because it will tell you whether the model is actually learning anything from the data.

For a full analysis of the model performance, you need to measure the performance of the model using the test set. This can be done by invoking the `test_minibatch` method on the `trainer` as follows:

```
trainer.test_minibatch( {features: X_test, label: y_test })
```

This method accepts a dictionary with a mapping between the input variables and the data for the variables. The output of this method is the output of the `metric` function you've configured earlier. In our case, it's the accuracy of our model based on the data we've given as input.

When the accuracy on the test set is higher than the accuracy on the training set, we will have a model that is underfitting. We're dealing with overfitting when the accuracy on the test set is lower than the accuracy on the training set.

Both underfitting and overfitting are bad if you take them too far. The best performance is achieved when the accuracy on both test set and training set are almost the same. We'll talk more about model performance in Chapter 4, *Validating Model Performance*.

Making predictions with a neural network

One of the most satisfying things after training a deep learning model is to actually use it in an application. For now, we'll limit ourselves to using the model with a sample that we randomly pick from our test set. But, later on, in Chapter 7, *Deploying Models to Production*, we'll look at how to save the model to disk and use it in C# or .NET to build applications with it.

Let's write the code to make a prediction with the neural network that we trained:

```
sample_index = np.random.choice(X_test.shape[0])
sample = X_test[sample_index]

inverted_mapping = {
    1: 'Iris-setosa',
    2: 'Iris-versicolor',
    3: 'Iris-virginica'
}

prediction = z(sample)
predicted_label = inverted_mapping[np.argmax(prediction)]

print(predicted_label)
```

Follow the given steps:

1. First, pick a random item from the test set using the np.random.choice function
2. Then select the sample data from the test set using the generated sample_index
3. Next, create an inverted mapping so you can convert the numeric output of the neural network to an actual label
4. Now, use the selected sample data and make a prediction by invoking the neural network z as a function

5. From the predicted output, take the index of the neuron that has the highest value as the predicted value using the `np.argmax` function from the `numpy` package

6. Use the `inverted_mapping` to convert the index value into the real label

When you execute the code sample, you will get output similar to this:

```
Iris-versicolor
```

Improving the model

You will quickly learn that building and training neural networks takes more than one attempt. Usually, the first version of your model will not work as well as you hope. It requires quite a bit of experimentation to come up with a great model.

A good neural network starts with a great dataset. In nearly all cases, better performance is achieved by using a proper dataset. Many data scientists will tell you that they spend about 80% of their time working on a good dataset. As with all computer software, if you put garbage in, you will get garbage out.

Even with a good dataset, you still need to spend quite some time to build and train different models before you get the performance you're after. So, let's see what you can do to improve your model after you've built it for the first time.

After you've trained the model for the first time, you have a couple of options to choose from in order to improve your model.

Take a look at the accuracy of your training and validation sets. Is the accuracy on the training set lower? Try to train the model for more epochs. Usually, this will help improve the model.

Does the training accuracy not improve even, if you train the model for longer? Then your model is probably unable to learn the complex relationships in your dataset. Try to change the model structure, and train the model again to see if that improves the accuracy.

For example, try to change the activation function or the number of neurons in your hidden layers. This will usually help the model to learn the more complex relationships in the dataset.

Alternatively, you can take a look at the number of layers in your model. Adding one more layer can have quite a large effect on the ability of your model to learn rules from the data you feed it.

Finally, when that doesn't help, take a look at the initialization of the layers in your model. In some cases, choosing a different initialization function helps the model during the initial learning steps.

The key to the process of experimentation is to change one thing at a time and keep track of your experiments. Using a source control solution such as Git can help you keep track of different versions of your training code.

Summary

In this chapter, we've built our first neural network and trained it to recognize iris flowers. While this sample is really basic, it shows how to use CNTK to build and train neural networks.

We've seen how to use the layer library in CNTK to our advantage to quickly define the structure for our neural network. In this chapter, we've talked about a few basic building blocks, such as the `Dense` layer and the `Sequential` layer, to chain several other layers together. In the coming chapters, we will learn other layer functions to build other types of neural networks such as convolutional networks.

In this chapter, we've also discussed how to use `learner` and `trainer` to build a basic algorithm to train our neural network. We've used the `train_minibatch` method, together with a basic loop, to construct our own training process. This is a pretty simple and powerful way to train our model. In the next chapter, we'll discuss other methods of training and the `train_minibatch` method in much more detail.

After we trained the model, we made use of the functional properties of CNTK to make a prediction with our trained model. The fact that a model is a function is quite powerful, and makes it really intuitive to use trained models in your application.

Finally, we've seen how to measure model performance using the `test_minibatch` method, and how to use performance metrics to check whether our model is overfitting. We later discussed how to use metrics to determine how to improve the model.

In the next chapter, we will look at different ways to access and feed data to CNTK models. We'll also explore each method of data access in CNTK, and which are the most appropriate to use in different circumstances.

Getting Data into Your Neural Network

3

There are many techniques you can use to load data to train a neural network or make predictions. What technique you use depends on how large your dataset is and in what format you've stored your data. In the previous chapter, we've seen how to feed data into a CNTK trainer manually. In this chapter, we will learn more ways to feed data into your neural network.

 The following topics will be covered in this chapter:

- Training your neural network efficiently with minibatches
- Working with small in-memory datasets
- Working with large datasets
- Taking control over the minibatch loop

Technical requirements

We assume you have a recent version of Anaconda installed on your computer and have followed the steps in Chapter 1, *Getting Started with CNTK*, to install CNTK on your computer. The sample code for this chapter can be found in our GitHub repository at `https://github.com/PacktPublishing/Deep-Learning-with-Microsoft-Cognitive-Toolkit-Quick-Start-Guide/tree/master/ch3`.

In this chapter, we'll work on a few examples stored in Jupyter notebooks. To access the sample code, run the following commands inside an Anaconda prompt in the directory where you've downloaded the code:

```
cd ch3
jupyter notebook
```

We'll mention the relevant notebooks in each of the sections so you can follow along and try out different techniques yourself.

Check out the following video to see the code in action:

```
http://bit.ly/2UczHuH
```

Training a neural network efficiently with minibatches

In the previous chapter, we discussed how to build and train a neural network. In this chapter, we'll discuss various ways to feed data to the CNTK trainer. Before we dive into the details of each data processing method, let's take a closer look at what happens with the data when you train a neural network.

You need a couple of things to train a neural network. As we discussed in the previous chapter, you need to have a basic structure for your model and a loss function. The trainer and the learner are the final pieces to the puzzle and are responsible for controlling the training process.

The trainer performs four steps:

1. It takes a number of training samples and feeds them through the network and loss function
2. Next, it takes the output of the loss function and feeds it through the learner
3. It then uses the learner to get a set of gradients for the parameters in the network
4. Finally, it uses the gradients to determine the new value of each parameter in the network

This process is repeated for all samples in your dataset to train the network for a full epoch. Usually, you need to train the network for multiple epochs to get the best result.

We previously only talked about single samples when training a neural network. But that is not what happens inside CNTK.

CNTK and many other frameworks use minibatches to train neural networks. A minibatch is a set of samples taken from your dataset. Essentially, a minibatch is a very small table of samples. It contains a predefined number of samples for the input features and an equal number of samples for the targets of your neural network.

The minibatch is passed through the network during training to calculate the output of the loss function. The output for the `loss` function is no longer a single value, but rather a list of values equal to the number of rows in the minibatch. This list of values is then passed through the `learner` to obtain a set of gradients for each of the parameters in the neural network.

Now, there's a problem with working with minibatches. We want one gradient per parameter to optimize its value. But we get a list of gradients instead. We can solve this by calculating the average over the gradients for each parameter. The average gradients are then used to update the parameters in the neural network.

Working with minibatches speeds up the training process but comes at a cost. Because we now have to deal with averages, we lose some resolution in calculating the gradients for the parameters in the model. It is quite possible to have a gradient of zero in a single minibatch as a result of averaging all the calculated gradients. When you use minibatches to train your neural network, you will get a lower quality model.

You need to set the number of samples per minibatch yourself before you start to train your neural network. Choosing a higher minibatch size will result in faster training at the cost of quality. A lower minibatch size is slower but produces better models. Choosing the right minibatch size is a matter of experimentation.

There's also a memory aspect to choosing the minibatch size. The minibatch size depends on how much memory you have available in your machine. You will find that you can fit fewer samples in the memory of your graphics card than you can in regular computer memory.

All methods described the next sections will use minibatches automatically. Later in the chapter, in the section, *Taking control over the minibatch loop,* we will discuss how to take control of the minibatch loop yourself should you need to.

Working with small in-memory datasets

There are many ways in which you can feed data to the CNTK trainer. Which technique you should use depends on the size of the dataset and the format of the data. Let's take a look at how to work with smaller in-memory datasets first.

When you work with in-memory data in Python you will most likely use a framework such as Pandas or NumPy. These frameworks work with vectors and matrices of floating point or object data at their core and offer various levels of convenience when it comes to working with data.

Let's go over each of these libraries and explore how you can use data stored in these libraries to train your neural network.

Working with numpy arrays

The first library we'll explore is numpy. Numpy is the most basic library available in Python for performing mathematical operations on n-dimensional arrays. It features an efficient way to store matrices and vectors in computer memory. The numpy library defines a large number of operators to manipulate these n-dimensional arrays. For example, it has built-in functions to calculate the average value over a whole matrix or rows/columns in a matrix.

You can follow along with any of the code in this section by opening the `Training using numpy arrays.ipynb` notebook in your browser using the instructions described at the start of this chapter.

Let's take a look at how to work with a numpy-based dataset in CNTK. As an example, we'll use a randomly generated dataset. We'll simulate data for a binary classification problem. Imagine that we have a set of observations with four features. We want to predict two possible labels with our model. First, we need to generate a set of labels that contain a one-hot vector representation of the labels that we want to predict. Next, we'll also need a set of features that will serve as the input features for our model:

```
import numpy as np

num_samples = 20000

label_mapping = np.eye(2)
y = label_mapping[np.random.choice(2,num_samples)].astype(np.float32)
X = np.random.random(size=(num_samples, 4)).astype(np.float32)
```

Follow the given steps:

1. First, import the `numpy` package under the `np` alias
2. Then, generate a `label` mapping using the `np.eye` function
3. After that, collect 20,000 random samples from the generated `label mapping` using the `np.random.choice` function
4. Finally, generate an array of random floating point values using the `np.random.random` function

The generated label mapping is a one-hot representation of the possible classes that we support and looks like this:

```
[0, 1]
[1, 0]
```

The generated matrices need to be converted to 32-bit floating point numbers in order to match the format expected by CNTK. Without this step, you will see an error telling you the format is not of the expected type. CNTK expects that you provide double-precision or float 32 data points.

Let's define a basic model that fits the dataset we just generated:

```
from cntk.layers import Dense, Sequential
from cntk import input_variable, default_options
from cntk.ops import sigmoid
from cntk.losses import binary_cross_entropy

with default_options(activation=sigmoid):
    model = Sequential([
        Dense(6),
        Dense(2)
    ])

features = input_variable(4)

z = model(features)
```

Follow the given steps:

1. First, import the `Dense` and `Sequential` layer function from the `layers` module
2. Then, import the `sigmoid` as the activation function for the layers in the network
3. After that, import the `binary_cross_entropy` function as the `loss` function to train the network

4. Next, define the default options for the network providing the `sigmoid` activation function as a default setting

5. Now, create the model using the `Sequential` layer function.

6. Use two `Dense` layers, one with 6 neurons and another one with 2 neurons which will serve as the output layer

7. Initialize an `input_variable` with 4 input features, which will serve as the input for the network.

8. Finally, connect the `features` variable to the neural network to complete it.

This model will have four inputs and two outputs matching the format of our randomly generated dataset. For demonstration purposes, we inserted an additional hidden layer with six neurons.

Now that we have a neural network, let's train it using our in-memory dataset:

```
from cntk.learners import sgd
from cntk.logging import ProgressPrinter

progress_writer = ProgressPrinter(0)

labels = input_variable(2)
loss = binary_cross_entropy(z, labels)
learner = sgd(z.parameters, lr=0.1)

training_summary = loss.train((X,y), parameter_learners=[learner],
callbacks=[progress_writer])
```

Follow the given steps:

1. First, import the `sgd` learner from the `learners` module

2. Next, import the `ProgressPrinter` from the `logging` module

3. Define a new `input_variable` for the labels

4. To train the model, define a `loss` using the `binary_cross_entropy` function and provide it the model `z` and the `labels` variable

5. Next, initialize the `sgd` learner and provide it with the parameters of the model and the `labels` variable

6. Finally, call the `train` method on the `loss` function and provide it with the input data, the `sgd` learner and the `progress_printer` as a callback

You're not required to provide callbacks for the `train` method. But it can be useful to plug in a progress writer so you can monitor the training process. Without this, you can't really see what is happening during training.

When you run the sample code, it will produce output similar to this:

average loss	since last	average metric	since last	examples
Learning rate per minibatch: 0.5				
1.4	1.4	0	0	512
1.4	1.4	0	0	1536
1.39	1.39	0	0	3584
1.39	1.39	0	0	7680
1.39	1.39	0	0	15872

It lists the learning average loss per minibatch, the loss since the last minibatch, and the metrics. Since we didn't provide metrics, the values in the metrics columns will remain 0. In the last column, the number of examples seen by the neural network is listed.

In the previous example, we've executed the `learner` with a default batch size. You can control the batch size using the `minibatch_size` keyword argument:

```
training_summary = loss.train((X,y),
    parameter_learners=[learner],
    callbacks=[progress_writer],
    minibatch_size=512)
```

Setting `minibatch_size` to a larger value will increase the speed of training but at the cost of a slightly worse model.

Try experimenting with different minibatch sizes in the sample code and see how it affects the performance of the model. Even with a model trained with random data.

Working with pandas DataFrames

Numpy arrays are the most basic way of storing data. Numpy arrays are very limited in what they can contain. A single n-dimensional array can contain data of a single data type. For many real-world cases, you need a library that can handle more than one data type in a single dataset. For example, you will find many datasets online where the label column is a string while the rest of the columns in the dataset contain floating point numbers.

The pandas library makes it easier to work with these kinds of datasets and is used by many developers and data scientists. It's a library that allows you to load datasets from disk stored in many different formats as DataFrames. For example, you can read DataFrames stored as JSON, CSV, and even Excel.

Pandas introduces the concept of a dataframe and with it introduces a large amount of mathematical and statistical functions that you can run against a data frame. Let's take a look at the structure of a pandas DataFrame to see how this library works:

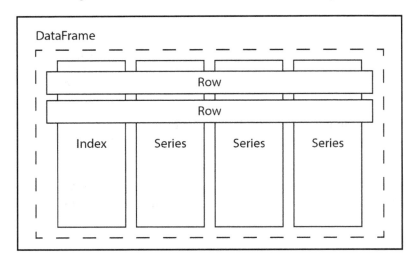

A DataFrame in pandas is a collection of series that define the individual columns. Each DataFrame also has an index that allows you to look up specific rows in the DataFrame by a key value stored in the index.

What makes a DataFrame unique is the large collection of methods defined on both the series and the dataset itself. For example, you can call describe on the DataFrame to get summary statistics for the whole DataFrame at once.

Invoking the describe method on a single series will get you the same summary statistics for that specific column in your DataFrame.

Pandas is widely used by data scientists and developers to work with data in Python. Because it is so widely used, it is good to know how to handle data stored in pandas with CNTK.

In the previous chapter, we've loaded a dataset that contains samples of Iris flowers and used that dataset to train a classification model. Before, we used a trainer instance to train the neural network. This is what happens too when you call train on a loss function. The train method will automatically create a trainer and a session for you so you don't have to do it manually.

In chapter 2, *Building Neural Networks with CNTK*, we talked about classifying three possible species of iris flowers based on four properties. You can either get the file from the sample code included with this book or by downloading the dataset from the UCI datasets archive at https://archive.ics.uci.edu/ml/datasets/Iris. Let's see how we can use the train method on the loss function to train the network that we created in the previous chapter:

```python
from cntk import default_options, input_variable
from cntk.layers import Dense, Sequential
from cntk.ops import log_softmax, sigmoid

model = Sequential([
    Dense(4, activation=sigmoid),
    Dense(3, activation=log_softmax)
])

features = input_variable(4)

z = model(features)
```

The model we used previously to classify flowers contains one hidden layer and an output layer with three neurons to match the number of classes we can predict.

In order to train the model, we need to load and preprocess the iris dataset so that it matches the expected layout and data format for the neural network:

```python
import numpy as np
import pandas as pd

df_source = pd.read_csv('iris.csv',
    names=['sepal_length', 'sepal_width','petal_length','petal_width',
'species'],
    index_col=False)

label_mapping = {
    'Iris-setosa': 0,
    'Iris-versicolor': 1,
    'Iris-virginica': 2
}

X = df_source.iloc[:, :4].values

y = df_source['species'].values
y = np.array([one_hot(label_mapping[v], 3) for v in y])

X = X.astype(np.float32)
y = y.astype(np.float32)
```

Follow the givens steps:

1. First, load the dataset into memory using the `read_csv` function
2. Next, create a dictionary mapping the labels in the dataset with their corresponding numeric representation
3. Select the first four columns using the `iloc` indexer on the `DataFrame`
4. Select the species columns as the labels for the dataset
5. Map the labels in the dataset using the `label_mapping` and use `one_hot` encoding to convert them into one-hot encoded arrays
6. Convert both the features and the mapped labels to floats so you can use them with CNTK

The labels are stored in the dataset as strings, CNTK can't work with these string values it needs one-hot encoded vectors representing the labels. To encode the labels we'll need to use the mapping table and the `one_hot` function which you can create using the following code:

```
def one_hot(index, length):
    result = np.zeros(length)
    result[index] = index
    return result
```

Follow the given steps:

1. Use the `np.zeros` function to create a new vector of size `length` and fill it with zeros
2. Select the element at the provided `index` and set its value to `1`
3. Return the `result` so it can be used in the dataset

Once we have the numpy arrays in the right format, we can use them as before to train our model:

```
from cntk.losses import cross_entropy_with_softmax
from cntk.learners import sgd
from cntk.logging import ProgressPrinter

progress_writer = ProgressPrinter(0)

labels = input_variable(3)
loss = cross_entropy_with_softmax(z, labels)
learner = sgd(z.parameters, 0.1)

train_summary = loss.train((X,y),
    parameter_learners=[learner],
```

```
callbacks=[progress_writer],
minibatch_size=16,
max_epochs=5)
```

Follow the given steps:

1. Import the `cross_entropy_with_softmax` function as the loss for the model.
2. Then, import the `sgd` learner to optimize the parameters.
3. After that, import the `ProgressPrinter` from the `logging` module to visualize the training progress.
4. Next, create a new instance of the `ProgressPrinter` to log the output of the optimizer.
5. Create a new `input_variable` to store the labels for training.
6. Initialize the `sgd` learner and give it the parameters of the model and a learning rate of `0.1`.
7. Finally, invoke the `train` method on the loss and feed it the training data, the `learner` and the `progress_writer`. In addition to this provide the `train` method with a `minibatch_size` of `16` and set the `max_epochs` keyword argument to `5`.

The `max_epochs` keyword argument for the `train` method on the `loss` function is optional. When you leave it out, the `trainer` will train the model for one epoch.

We're using `ProgressWriter` to generate output from the training process so we can monitor the progress of the training session. You can leave this out, but it's a great help to get a sense of what is happening during training. With the progress writer configured, the output will look similar to this:

average loss	since last	average metric	since last	examples
Learning rate per minibatch: 0.1				
1.1	1.1	0	0	16
0.835	0.704	0	0	48
0.993	1.11	0	0	112
1.14	1.14	0	0	16
0.902	0.783	0	0	48
1.03	1.13	0	0	112
1.19	1.19	0	0	16
0.94	0.817	0	0	48
1.06	1.16	0	0	112
1.14	1.14	0	0	16
0.907	0.79	0	0	48

1.05	1.15	0	0	112
1.07	1.07	0	0	16
0.852	0.744	0	0	48
1.01	1.14	0	0	112

Since we're using the same method to train the network as with regular numpy arrays, we can control the batch size too. We'll leave it up to you to try different settings for the batch size and discover what produces the best model.

Working with large datasets

We've looked at NumPy and Pandas as ways to feed in-memory dataset to CNTK for training. But not every dataset is small enough to fit into memory. This is especially true for datasets that contain images, video samples, or sound samples. When you work with larger datasets, you only want to load small portions of the dataset at a time into memory. Usually, you will only load enough samples into memory to run a single minibatch of training.

CNTK supports working with larger datasets through the use of MinibatchSource. Now, MinibatchSource is a component that can load data from disk in chunks. It can automatically randomize samples read from the data source. This is useful for preventing your neural network from overfitting due to a fixed order in the training dataset.

MinibatchSource has a built-in transformation pipeline. You can use this pipeline to augment your data. This is a useful feature when you work with data such as images. When you are training a model based on images, you want to make sure that an image is recognized even at a funny angle. The transformation pipeline allows you to generate extra samples by rotating the original images read from disk.

A unique feature of MinibatchSource is that it loads data on a background thread separate from the training process. By loading data in a separate thread, it can load minibatches ahead of time so that your graphics card doesn't get stalled on this process.

In this chapter, we'll limit ourselves to the basic usage of MinibatchSource. In Chapter 5, *Working with Images*, and Chapter 6, *Working with Time Series Data*, we'll look at how you can use the MinibatchSource component with images and time series data.

Let's explore how to use a minibatch source with out-of-memory data to work with larger datasets and use it to feed data for training a neural network.

Creating a MinibatchSource instance

In the section, *Working with pandas DataFrames,* we worked on the iris flower example. Let's go back and replace the code that uses data from a pandas DataFrame with MinibatchSource. The first step is to create a basic MinibatchSource instance:

```
from cntk.io import StreamDef, StreamDefs, MinibatchSource,
CTFDeserializer, INFINITELY_REPEAT

labels_stream = StreamDef(field='labels', shape=3, is_sparse=False)
features_stream = StreamDef(field='features', shape=4, is_sparse=False)

deserializer = CTFDeserializer('iris.ctf', StreamDefs(labels=labels_stream,
features=features_stream))

minibatch_source = MinibatchSource(deserializer, randomize=True)
```

Follow the given steps:

1. First, import the components for the minibatch source from the io module.
2. Next, create a stream definition for the labels using the StreamDef class. Use the labels field and set it to read 3 features from the stream. Make sure to use the is_sparse keyword argument and set it to False.
3. Then, create another StreamDef instance and read the features field from the input file. This stream has 4 features. Use the is_sparse keyword argument to specify that the data is stored as dense vectors.
4. After that, initialize the deserializer. Provide the iris.ctf file as the input and feed it the stream definitions by wrapping them in a StreamDefs instance.
5. Finally, create a MinibatchSource instance using the deserializer.

Creating CTF files

The data that we're using comes from the file iris.ctf and is stored in a file format called **CNTK Text Format (CTF)**. This is a file format that looks like this:

```
|features 0.1 2.0 3.1 5.4 |labels 0 1 0
|features 2.3 4.1 5.1 5.2 |labels 1 0 1
```

Each line contains a single sample for our neural network. Each line can contain values for multiple inputs of our model. Each input is preceded by a vertical pipe. The values for each input are separated by a space.

The CTFDeserializer can read the file by using the stream definitions that we initialized in the code sample.

In order to get the data for the MinibatchSource instance we just created, you need to create a CTF file for our dataset. There's no official converter to turn data formats such as **Comma-Separated Value** (**CSV**) into CTF files, so you need to write some Python code. You can find the code to prepare a CTF file for training with a minibatch size in the Creating a CTF file.ipynb notebook in the sample code for this chapter.

Let's explore how to create a CTF file using Python. The first step is to load the data into memory and convert it to the correct format:

```python
import pandas as pd
import numpy as np

df_source = pd.read_csv('iris.csv',
    names=['sepal_length', 'sepal_width','petal_length','petal_width',
'species'],
    index_col=False)


features = df_source.iloc[:,:4].values
labels = df_source['species'].values

label_mapping = {
    'Iris-setosa': 0,
    'Iris-versicolor': 1,
    'Iris-virginica': 2
}

labels = [one_hot(label_mapping[v], 3) for v in labels]
```

Follow the given steps:

1. Before we start to process the data, import the pandas and numpy packages to get access to the data processing functions.
2. First, load the iris.csv file into memory and store it in the df_source variable.
3. Then, take the contents of the first four columns using the iloc indexer as the features.
4. Next, use the data from species column as the labels for our dataset.
5. Now create a label_mapping dictionary to create a mapping between the label name and its numeric representation.
6. Finally, convert the labels to a set of one-hot encoded vectors using a Python list comprehension and the one_hot function.

To encode the labels we'll use a utility function called `one_hot` that you can create using the following code:

```
def one_hot(index, length):
    result = np.zeros(length)
    result[index] = 1
    return result
```

Follow the given steps:

1. Generate a new empty vector with the specified `length` using the `np.zeros` function
2. Next, take the element at the specified `index` and set it to 1
3. Finally, return the newly generated one-hot encoded vector so you can use it in the rest of your code

Once we have loaded and preprocessed the data, we can store it on disk in the CTF file format:

```
with open('iris.ctf', 'w') as output_file:
    for index in range(0, features.shape[0]):
        feature_values = ' '.join([str(x) for x in
np.nditer(features[index])])
        label_values = ' '.join([str(x) for x in np.nditer(labels[index])])
        output_file.write('|features {} |labels
{}\n'.format(feature_values, label_values))
```

Follow the given steps:

1. First, we open the `iris.ctf` file for writing
2. Then, iterate over all the records in the dataset
3. For each record, create a new string containing the serialized values for the `features` vector
4. Next, serialize the `labels` to a string using a Python list comprehension
5. Finally, write the `features` and `labels` to the file

The elements in the `features` and `labels` vector should be separated by a space. Note that each of the serialized pieces of data gets prefixed by a pipe-character and its name in the output file.

Feeding data into a training session

To train with `MinibatchSource`, we can use the same training logic as before. Only this time, we'll use `MinibatchSource` as the input for the `train` method on the `loss` function:

```
from cntk.logging import ProgressPrinter
from cntk.train import Trainer, training_session

minibatch_size = 16
samples_per_epoch = 150
num_epochs = 30

input_map = {
    features: minibatch_source.streams.features,
    labels: minibatch_source.streams.labels
}

progress_writer = ProgressPrinter(0)

train_history = loss.train(minibatch_source,
        parameter_learners=[learner],
        model_inputs_to_streams=input_map,
        callbacks=[progress_writer],
        epoch_size=samples_per_epoch,
        max_epochs=num_epochs)
```

Follow the given steps:

1. First, import the `ProgressPrinter` so we can log the output of the training session.
2. Next, import the `trainer` and the `training_session`, you'll need these to set up the training session.
3. Then, define a set of constants for the training code. The `minibatch_size` to control the number of samples per batch, `samples_per_epoch` to control the number of samples in a single epoch and finally the `num_epochs` setting to control the number of epochs to train for.
4. Define a mapping between the input variables for the network and the streams in the minibatch source so CNTK knows how to read data during training.
5. Then, initialize the `progress_writer` variable with a new `ProgressPrinter` instance to log the output of the training process.
6. Finally, invoke the `train` method on the `loss` providing the `MinibatchSource` and the `input_map` in the `model_inputs_to_stream` keyword argument.

You can run the code from this section when you open `Training with a minibatch source.ipynb` from the sample code for this chapter. We've included a `progress printer` instance to visualize the output of the training session. When you run the code, you will get output similar to this:

```
average  since  average  since  examples
loss     last   metric   last
-------------------------------------------------------
Learning rate per minibatch: 0.1
1.21     1.21   0        0      32
1.15     1.12   0        0      96
1.09     1.09   0        0      32
1.03     1.01   0        0      96
0.999    0.999  0        0      32
0.999    0.998  0        0      96
0.972    0.972  0        0      32
0.968    0.966  0        0      96
0.928    0.928  0        0      32
[...]
```

Taking control over the minibatch loop

In the previous section, we've seen how to use the CTF format with `MinibatchSource` to feed data to the CNTK trainer. But most datasets don't come in this format. So, you can't really use this format unless you create your own dataset or convert the original dataset to the CTF format.

CNTK currently supports a limited set of `deserializers` for images, text, and speech. You can't extend the deserializers at the moment, which limits what you can do with the standard `MinibatchSource`. You can create your own `UserMinibatchSource`, but this is a complicated process. So, instead of showing you how to build a custom `MinibatchSource`, let's look at how to feed data into the CNTK trainer manually.

Let's first recreate the model we used to classify Iris flowers:

```
from cntk import default_options, input_variable
from cntk.layers import Dense, Sequential
from cntk.ops import log_softmax, sigmoid

model = Sequential([
    Dense(4, activation=sigmoid),
    Dense(3, activation=log_softmax)
])
```

```
features = input_variable(4)

z = model(features)
```

The model remains the same as in previous sections; it is a basic classification model with four input neurons and three output neurons. We'll be using a categorical cross-entropy loss since this is a multi-class classification problem.

Let's train the model using a manual minibatch loop:

```
import pandas as pd
import numpy as np
from cntk.losses import cross_entropy_with_softmax
from cntk.logging import ProgressPrinter
from cntk.learners import sgd
from cntk.train import Trainer

labels = input_variable(3)
loss = cross_entropy_with_softmax(z, labels)
learner = sgd(z. parameters, 0.1)

progress_writer = ProgressPrinter(0)
trainer = Trainer(z, (loss, None), learner, progress_writer)

input_data = pd.read_csv('iris.csv',
    names=['sepal_length', 'sepal_width','petal_length','petal_width',
'species'],
    index_col=False, chunksize=16)

for df_batch in input_data:
    feature_values = df_batch.iloc[:,:4].values
    feature_values = feature_values.astype(np.float32)
    label_values = df_batch.iloc[:,-1]
    label_values = label_values.map(lambda x: label_mapping[x])
    label_values = label_values.values

    encoded_labels = np.zeros((label_values.shape[0], 3))
    encoded_labels[np.arange(label_values.shape[0]), label_values] = 1.

    trainer.train_minibatch({features: feature_values, labels:
encoded_labels})
```

Follow the given steps:

1. First, import the components needed for training the neural network.
2. Next, define an `input _variable` to store the labels.

3. Then, define the `loss` function using the `cross_entropy_with_softmax` function and connect the output of the neural network and the labels variable to it.

4. After that, initialize the `learner` with the parameters of the neural network and a learning rate of `0.1`.

5. Create a new instance of the `ProgressWriter` to log the output of the training process.

6. Next, create a new instance of the `Trainer` class and initialize it with the network, the `loss`, the `learner` and the `progress_writer`.

7. After you've initialized the network, Load the dataset from disk and use the `chunksize` keyword argument so it is read in chunks rather than loading the dataset into memory in one operation.

8. Now create a new `for` loop to iterate over the chunks of the dataset.

9. Process each chunk by extracting the `labels` and `features` from it in the appropriate format. Use the first four columns as the input features for the neural network and the last column as the labels.

10. Convert the label values to one-hot encoded vectors using the `one_hot` function from the section *Working with pandas DataFrames*.

11. Finally, call the `train_minibatch` method on the `trainer` and feed it the `features` and `labels`.

Note that we didn't write any code to run multiple epochs of training. If you want, you can introduce this into the code by wrapping the logic for reading and processing minibatches from the CSV file in another `for` loop. Check out the `Training with a manual minibatch loop.ipynb` notebook in the sample code for this chapter to give it a try.

You will find that preparing a single minibatch is a lot more work with a manual minibatch loop. This comes mainly from the fact that we're not using the automatic chunking that comes with the standard `MinibatchSource` logic. Also, since we haven't preprocessed the dataset beforehand, we need to encode the labels during training.

When you have to work with a large dataset and can't use `MinibatchSource`, a manual minibatch loop is your last resort. It is, however, much more powerful because you get a lot more control over how your model is trained. Using a manual minibatch loop can be very useful if you want to perform complex operations on each minibatch or change settings as the training progresses.

Summary

In this chapter, we've explored how you can train your neural networks with both small and large datasets. For smaller datasets, we've looked at how you can quickly train a model by calling the `train` method on the `loss` function. For larger datasets, we've explored how you can use both `MinibatchSource` and a manual minibatch loop to train your network.

Using the right method of training can make a big difference in how long it takes to train your model and how good your model will be in the end. You can now make an informed choice between using in-memory data and reading data in chunks. Make sure you experiment with the minibatch size settings to see what works best for your model.

Up until this chapter, we haven't looked at methods to monitor your model. We did see some fragments with a progress writer to help you visualize the training process. But that's pretty limited.

In the next chapter, we'll learn how to measure the performance of neural networks. We'll also explore how to monitor and debug CNTK models using different visualization and monitoring tools.

Validating Model Performance 4

When you've built a deep learning model using neural networks, you are left with the question of how well it can predict when presented with new data. Are the predictions made by the model accurate enough to be usable in a real-world scenario? In this chapter, we will look at how to measure the performance of your deep learning models. We'll also dive into tooling to monitor and debug your models.

By the end of this chapter, you'll have a solid understanding of different validation techniques you can use to measure the performance of your model. You'll also know how to use a tool such as TensorBoard to get into the details of your neural network. Finally, you will know how to apply different visualizations to debug your neural network.

The following topics will be covered in this chapter:

- Choosing a good strategy to validate model performance
- Validating the performance of a classification model
- Validating the performance of a regression model
- Measuring performance of a for out-of-memory datasets
- Monitoring your model

Technical requirements

We assume you have a recent version of Anaconda installed on your computer and have followed the steps in Chapter 1, *Getting Started with CNTK*, to install CNTK on your computer. The sample code for this chapter can be found in our GitHub repository at https://github.com/PacktPublishing/Deep-Learning-with-Microsoft-Cognitive-Toolkit-Quick-Start-Guide/tree/master/ch4.

In this chapter, we'll work on a few examples stored in Jupyter Notebooks. To access the sample code, run the following commands inside an Anaconda prompt in the directory where you've downloaded the code:

```
cd ch4
jupyter notebook
```

We'll mention relevant notebooks in each of the sections so you can follow along and try out different techniques yourself.

Check out the following video to see the code in action:

```
http://bit.ly/2TVuoR3
```

Choosing a good strategy to validate model performance

Before we dive into different validation techniques for various kinds of models, let's talk a little bit about validating deep learning models in general.

When you build a machine learning model, you're training it with a set of data samples. The machine learning model learns these samples and derives general rules from them. When you feed the same samples to the model, it will perform pretty well on those samples. However, when you feed new samples to the model that you haven't used in training, the model will behave differently. It will most likely be worse at making a good prediction on those samples. This happens because your model will always tend to lean toward data it has seen before.

But we don't want our model to be good at predicting the outcome for samples it has seen before. It needs to work well for samples that are new to the model, because in a production environment you will get different input that you need to predict an outcome for. To make sure that our model works well, we need to validate it using a set of samples that we didn't use for training.

Let's take a look at two different techniques for creating a dataset for validating a neural network. First, we'll explore how to use a hold-out dataset. After that we'll focus on a more complex method of creating a separate validation dataset.

Using a hold-out dataset for validation

The first and easiest method to create a dataset to validate a neural network is to use a hold-out set. You're holding back one set of samples from training and using those samples to measure the performance of your model after you're done training the model:

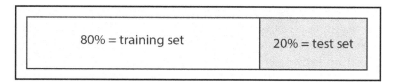

The ratio between training and validation samples is usually around 80% training samples versus 20% test samples. This ensures that you have enough data to train the model and a reasonable amount of samples to get a good measurement of the performance.

Usually, you choose random samples from the main dataset to include in the training and test set. This ensures that you get an even distribution between the sets.

You can produce your own hold-out set using the `train_test_split` function from the `scikit-learn` library. It accepts any number of datasets and splits them into two segments based on either the `train_size` or the `test_size` keyword parameter:

```
from sklearn.model_selection import train_test_split

X_train, X_test, y_train, y_test = train_test_split(X, y, test_size=0.2)
```

It is good practice to randomly split your dataset each time you run a training session. Deep learning algorithms, such as the ones used in CNTK, are highly influenced by random-number generators, and the order in which you provide samples to the neural network during training. So, to even out the effect of the sample order, you need to randomize the order of your dataset each time you train the model.

Using a hold-out set works well when you want to quickly measure the performance of your model. It's also great when you have a large dataset or a model that takes a long time to train. But there are downsides to using the hold-out technique.

Your model is sensitive to the order in which samples were provided during training. Also, each time you start a new training session, the random-number generator in your computer will provide different values to initialize the parameters in your neural network. This can cause swings in performance metrics. Sometimes, you will get really good results, but sometimes you get really bad results. In the end, this is bad because it is unreliable.

Be careful when randomizing datasets that contain sequences of samples that should be handled as a single input, such as when working with a time series dataset. Libraries such as `scikit-learn` don't handle this kind of dataset correctly and you may need to write your own randomization logic.

Using k-fold cross-validation

You can increase the reliability of the performance metrics for your model by using a technique called k-fold cross-validation. Cross-validation performs the same technique as the hold-out set. But it does it a number of times—usually about 5 to 10 times:

The process of k-fold cross-validation works like this: First, you split the dataset into a training and test set. You then train the model using the training set. Finally, you use the test set to calculate the performance metrics for your model. This process then gets repeated as many times as needed—usually 5 to 10 times. At the end of the cross-validation process, the average is calculated over all the performance metrics, which gives you the final performance metrics. Most tools will also give you the individual values so you can see how much variation there is between different training runs.

Cross-validation gives you a much more stable performance measurement, because you use a more realistic training and test scenario. The order of samples isn't defined in production, which is simulated by running the same training process a number of times. Also, we're using separate hold-out sets to simulate unseen data.

Using k-fold cross-validation takes a lot of time when validating deep learning models, so use it wisely. If you're still experimenting with the setup of your model, you're better off using the basic hold-out technique. Later, when you're done experimenting, you can use k-fold cross-validation to make sure that the model performs well in a production environment.

Note that CNTK doesn't include support for running k-fold cross-validation. You need to write your own scripts to do so.

What about underfitting and overfitting?

When you start to collect metrics for a neural network using either a hold-out dataset or by applying k-fold cross-validation you'll discover that the output for the metrics will be different for the training dataset and the validation dataset. In the this section, we'll take a look at how to use the information from the collected metrics to detect overfitting and underfitting problems for your model.

When a model is overfit, it performs really well on samples it has seen during training, but not on samples that are new. You can detect overfitting during validation by looking at the metrics. Your model is overfit when the metric on the test set is lower than the same metric on your training set.

A lot of overfitting is bad for business, since your model doesn't understand how to process new samples. But it is logical to have a little bit of overfitting in your model; this is expected, as you want to maximize the learning effort for your model.

The problem of overfitting becomes bigger when your model is trained on a dataset that doesn't represent the real-world environment it is used in. Then you end up with a model that is overfit toward the dataset. It will predict random output on new samples. Sadly, you can't detect this kind of overfitting. The only way to discover this problem is to use your model in production and use proper logging and user feedback to measure how well your model is doing.

Like overfitting, you can also have a model that is underfit. This means the model didn't learn enough from the training set and doesn't predict useful output. You can easily detect this with a performance metric. Usually, it will be lower than you anticipated. Actually, your model will be underfitting when you start training the first epoch and will become less underfit as training progresses.

Once the model is trained, it can still be underfit. You can detect this by looking at the metrics for the training set and the test set. When the metric on the test set is higher than the metric on the training set, you have an underfit model. You can fix this by looking carefully at the settings of your model and changing them so it becomes better the next time you train the model. You can also try to train it for a little longer to see whether that helps.

Monitoring tools will help to detect underfitting and overfitting of your model. So, make sure you use them. We'll talk about how to use them with CNTK later in the section *Monitoring your model.*

Validating performance of a classification model

In the previous section, *Choosing a good strategy to validate model performance*, we talked about choosing a good strategy for validating your neural network. In the following sections, we'll dive into choosing metrics for different kinds of models.

When you're building a classification model, you're looking for metrics that express how many samples were correctly classified. You're probably also interested in measuring how many samples were incorrectly classified.

You can use a confusion matrix—a table with the predicted output versus the expected output—to find out a lot of detail about the performance of your model. This tends to get complicated, so we'll also look at a way to measure the performance of a model using the F-measure.

Using a confusion matrix to validate your classification model

Let's take a closer look at how you can measure the performance of a classification model using a confusion matrix. To understand how a confusion matrix works, let's create a confusion matrix for a binary classification model that predicts whether a credit card transaction was normal or fraudulent:

	Actual fraud	Actual normal
Predicted fraud	True positive	False positive
Predicted normal	False negative	True negative

The sample confusion matrix contains two columns and two rows. We have a column for the class fraud and a column for the class normal. We've added rows to the fraud and normal classes as well. The cells in the table will contain numbers that tell us how many samples were marked as true positive, true negative, false positive, and false negative.

When the model correctly predicts fraud for a transaction, we're dealing with a true positive. When we predict fraud but the transaction should not have been marked as fraud, we're dealing with a false positive.

You can calculate a number of different things from the confusion matrix. First, you can calculate precision based on the values in the confusion matrix:

$$Precision = \frac{TruePositive}{TruePositive + FalsePositive}$$

Precision tells you how many samples were correctly predicted out of all the samples that we predicted. High precision means that your model suffers from very few false positives.

The second metric that we can calculate based on the confusion matrix is the recall metric:

$$Recall = \frac{TruePositive}{TruePositive + FalseNegative}$$

Recall tells you how many of the fraud cases in the dataset were actually detected by the model. Having a high recall means that your model is good at finding fraud cases in general.

Finally, you can calculate the overall accuracy of the model:

$$Accuracy = \frac{TruePositive}{TruePositive + TrueNegative + FalsePositive + FalseNegative}$$

The overall accuracy tells you how well the model does as a whole. But this is a dangerous metric to use when your dataset is unbalanced. For example: if you have 100 samples of which 5 are marked as fraud and 95 are marked as normal, predicting normal for all samples gives you an accuracy of *0.95*. This seems high, but we're fooling ourselves.

It's much better to calculate a balanced accuracy. For this, we need to know the precision and specificity of the model. We already know how to calculate the precision of our model. We can calculate the specificity using the following formula:

$$Specificity = \frac{TrueNegative}{TrueNegative + FalseNegative}$$

The specificity tells us how good our model is at detecting that a sample is normal instead of fraud. It is the perfect inverse of the precision, which tells us how good our model is at detecting fraud.

Once we have the specificity, we can combine it with the precision metric to calculate the balanced accuracy:

$$BalancedAccuracy = \frac{Precision + Specificity}{2}$$

The balanced accuracy tells us how good our model is at separating the dataset into fraud and normal cases, which is exactly what we want. Let's go back to our previous accuracy measurement and retry it using the balanced version of the accuracy metric:

$$\frac{0.0 + 0.95}{2} = 0.475$$

Remember, we had 100 samples, of which 5 should be marked as fraud. When we predict everything as normal, we end up with a precision of *0.0* because we didn't predict any fraud case correctly. The specificity is *0.95* because out of 100 samples we predicted 5 incorrectly as normal. The end result is a balanced accuracy of *0.475*, which is not very high, for obvious reasons.

Now that you have a good feel for what a confusion matrix looks like and how it works, let's talk about the more complex cases. When you have a multi-class classification model with more than two classes, you will need to expand the matrix with more rows and columns.

For example: when we create a confusion matrix for a model that predicts three possible classes, we could end up with the following:

	Actual A	Actual B	Actual C
Predicted A	91	75	60
Predicted B	5	15	30
Predicted C	4	10	10

We can still calculate the precision, recall, and specificity for this matrix. But it is more complex to do so, and we can only do it on a per-class basis. For example: when you want to calculate the precision for class A, you need to take the true positive rate of A, which is *91*, and divide it by the number of samples that were actually A but were predicted as B and C, which is *9* in total. This gives us the following calculation:

$$Precision = \frac{TruePositive}{TruePositive + FalsePositive} = \frac{91}{91 + 9} = 0.91$$

The process is much the same for calculating recall, specificity, and accuracy. To get an overall figure for the metrics, you need to calculate the average over all classes.

There are two strategies that you can follow to calculate the average metric, such as precision, recall, specificity, and accuracy. You can either choose to calculate the micro-average or the macro-average. Let's first explore the macro-average using the precision metric:

$$Precision_{macro} = \frac{Precision_A + Precision_B + Precision_C}{k}$$

To get the macro-average for the precision metric, we first add up the precision values for all classes and then divide them over the number of classes, *k*. The macro-average doesn't take into account any class imbalances. For example: there could be 100 samples for class A while there are only 20 samples for class B. Calculating the macro-average gives you a skewed picture.

When you work on multi-class classification models, it's better to use the micro-average for the different metrics—precision, recall, specificity, and accuracy. Let's take a look at how to calculate the micro-average precision:

$$Precision_{micro} = \frac{TP_A + TP_B + TP_C}{TP_A + TP_B + TP_C + FP_A + FP_B + FP_C}$$

First, we'll add up all the true positives for every class. We then divide them by the sum of all true positives and false negatives for every class. This will give us a much more balanced view of the different metrics.

Using the F-measure as an alternative to the confusion matrix

While using precision and recall give you a good idea of how your model performs, they can't be maximized at the same time. There's a strong relationship between the two metrics:

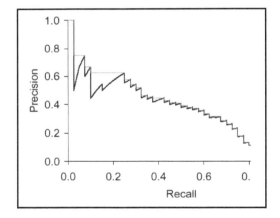

Let's see how this relationship between precision and recall plays out. Let's say you want to use a deep learning model to classify cell samples as cancerous or normal. In theory, to reach maximum precision in your model, you need to reduce the number of predictions to 1. This gives you the maximum chance to reach 100% precision, but recall becomes really low, as you're missing a lot of possible cases of cancer. When you want to reach maximum recall to detect as many cases of cancer as possible, you need to make as many predictions as possible. But this reduces precision, as you increase the chance that you get false positives.

In practice, you will find yourself balancing between precision and recall. Whether you should go primarily for precision or recall is dependent on what you want your model to predict. Often, you will need to talk to the user of your model to determine what they find most important: a low number of false positives or a high chance of finding that one patient who has a deadly disease.

Once you have made a choice between precision and recall, you need a way to express this in a metric. The F-measure allows you to do this. The F-measure expresses a harmonic average between precision and recall:

$$FMeasure = (1 + B^2)\frac{precision * recall}{B^2 * precision + recall}$$

The full formula for the F-measure includes an extra term, *B*, which is set to 1 to get an equal ratio of precision and recall. This is called the F1-measure and is the standard in almost all tools you will come across. It gives equal weight to recall and precision. When you want to emphasize recall, you can set the *B* factor to 2. Alternatively, when you want to emphasize precision in your model, you can set the *B* factor to 0.5.

In the next section, we'll see how to use the confusion matrix and f-measure in CNTK to measure the performance of a classification model.

Measuring classification performance in CNTK

Let's take a look at how you can use the CNTK metrics functions to create a confusion matrix for the flower classification model that we used in Chapter 2, *Building Neural Networks with CNTK*.

You can follow along with the code in this section by opening the `Validating performance of classification models.ipynb` notebook file from the sample files for this chapter. We'll focus on the validation code in this section. The sample code contains more detail on how to preprocess the data for the model as well.

Before we can train and validate the model, we'll need to prepare the dataset for training. We'll split the dataset into separate training and test sets to ensure that we get a proper performance measurement for our model:

```
from sklearn.model_selection import train_test_split

X_train, X_test, y_train, y_test = train_test_split(X,y, test_size=0.2,
stratify=y)
```

First, we'll import the `train_test_split` function from the `sklearn.model_selection` package. We then take the features, X, and the labels, y, and run them through the function to split them. We'll use 20% of the samples for testing.

Note that we're using the `stratify` keyword parameter. Because we're validating a classification model, we want to have a good balance between classes in the test and training set. Each class should ideally be equally represented in both the test and training set. When you feed a list of classes or labels to the `stratify` keyword, `scikit-learn` will take them to evenly distribute the samples over the training and test set.

Now that we have the training and test set, let's train the model:

```
from cntk.losses import cross_entropy_with_softmax
from cntk.learners import sgd
from cntk.logging import ProgressPrinter

progress_writer = ProgressPrinter(0)
loss = cross_entropy_with_softmax(z, labels)
learner = sgd(z.parameters, 0.1)

train_summary = loss.train((X_train,y_train),
                           parameter_learners=[learner],
                           callbacks=[progress_writer],
                           minibatch_size=16, max_epochs=15)
```

We'll run the whole dataset through the training function for a total of 15 epochs of training. We've included a progress writer to visualize the training process.

At this point, we don't know what the performance is like. We know that the loss decreased nicely over 15 epochs of training. But the question is this, is it enough? Let's find out by running the validation samples through the model and create a confusion matrix:

```
from sklearn.metrics import confusion_matrix

y_true = np.argmax(y_test, axis=1)
y_pred = np.argmax(z(X_test), axis=1)

matrix = confusion_matrix(y_true=y_true, y_pred=y_pred)

print(matrix)
```

We're using the `confusion_matrix` function from `scikit-learn` to create the confusion matrix. This function needs the true labels and the predicted labels. Both need to be stored as a numpy array with numeric values representing the labels. We don't have those numbers. We have a binary representation of the labels because that is what is required by the model. To fix this, we need to convert the binary representation of the labels into a numeric one. You can do this by invoking the `argmax` function from the `numpy` package. The output of the `confusion_matrix` function is a numpy array and looks like this:

```
[[ 8  0  0]
 [ 0  4  6]
 [ 0  0 10]]
```

We get three rows and three columns in the confusion matrix because we have three possible classes that our model can predict. The output itself isn't very pleasant to read. You can convert this table into a heat map using another package called `seaborn`:

```
import seaborn as sns
import matplotlib.pyplot as plt

g = sns.heatmap(matrix,
                annot=True,
                xticklabels=label_encoder.classes_.tolist(),
                yticklabels=label_encoder.classes_.tolist(),
                cmap='Blues')

g.set_yticklabels(g.get_yticklabels(), rotation=0)

g.set_xlabel('Predicted species')
g.set_ylabel('Actual species')
g.set_title('Confusion matrix for iris prediction model')

plt.show()
```

First, we create a new heat map based on the confusion matrix. We pass in the classes of the `label_encoder` used while preprocessing the dataset for the row and column labels.

The standard heat map needs some tweaks to be easily readable. We're using a custom colormap for the heat map. We're also using custom labels on the X and Y axes. Finally, we add a title and display the graph:

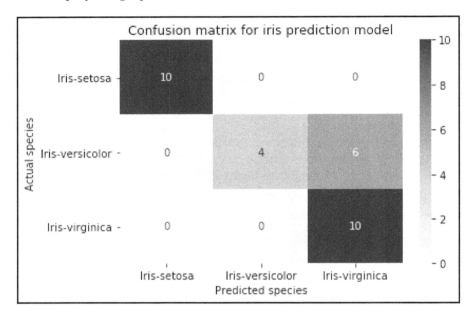

Standard heat map

Looking at the confusion matrix, you can quickly see how the model is doing. In this case, the model is missing quite a few cases for the Iris-versicolor class. Only 60% of the flowers of this species were correctly classified.

While the confusion matrix gives a lot of detail about how the model performs on different classes, it may be useful to get a single performance figure for your model so you can easily compare different experiments.

One way to get a single performance figure is to use the `classification_error` metric from CNTK. It calculates the fraction of samples that were misclassified.

To use it, we need to modify the training code. Instead of just having a `loss` function to optimize the model, we're going to include a metric as well. Previously we created just a `loss` function instance, this time we're going to have to write a `criterion` function that produces a combined `loss` and `metric` function that we can use during training. The following code demonstrates how to do this:

```
import cntk

@cntk.Function
def criterion_factory(output, target):
    loss = cntk.losses.cross_entropy_with_softmax(output, target)
    metric = cntk.metrics.classification_error(output, target)
    return loss, metric
```

Follow the given steps:

1. First, create a new Python function that takes our model as the `output` argument and the target that we want to optimize for as the `output` argument.
2. Within the function, create a `loss` function and provide it the `output` and `target`.
3. Next, create a `metric` function and provide it the `output` and `target` as well.
4. At the end of the function, return both as a tuple, where the first element is the `loss` function and the second element is the `metric` function.
5. Mark the function with `@cntk.Function`. This will wrap the loss and metric so we can call the `train` method on it to train the model and call the `test` method to validate the model.

Once we have the combined `loss` and `metric` function factory, we can use it during training:

```
from cntk.losses import cross_entropy_with_softmax
from cntk.learners import sgd
from cntk.logging import ProgressPrinter

progress_writer = ProgressPrinter(0)
loss = criterion_factory(z, labels)
learner = sgd(z.parameters, 0.1)

train_summary = loss.train((X_train,y_train),
                           parameter_learners=[learner],
                           callbacks=[progress_writer],
                           minibatch_size=16, max_epochs=15)
```

Follow the given steps:

1. First, import the `cross_entropy_with_softmax` function from the `losses` module
2. Next, import the `sgd` learner from the `learners` module
3. Also, import the `ProgressPrinter` from the `logging` module so you can log the output of the training process
4. Then, create a new instance `progress_writer` to log the output of the training process
5. Afer that, create a `loss` using the newly created `criterion_factory` function and feed it the model variable `z` and the `labels` variable
6. Next, create the `learner` instance using the `sgd` function and feed it the parameters and a learning rate of `0.1`
7. Finally, call the `train` method with the training data, the `learner` and the `progress_writer`

When we call train on the `loss` function, we get a slightly different output. Instead of just the loss, we also get to see the output of the `metric` function during training. In our case, the value of the metric should increase over time:

average loss	since last	average metric	since last	examples
Learning rate per minibatch: 0.1				
1.48	1.48	0.75	0.75	16
1.18	1.03	0.75	0.75	48
0.995	0.855	0.518	0.344	112
1.03	1.03	0.375	0.375	16
0.973	0.943	0.396	0.406	48
0.848	0.753	0.357	0.328	112
0.955	0.955	0.312	0.312	16
0.904	0.878	0.375	0.406	48

Finally, when we're done training, you can use the `test` method on the `loss/metric` combination function to calculate classification error using the test set we created earlier:

```
loss.test((X_test, y_test))
```

When you execute the `test` method on the `loss` function with a dataset, CNTK will take the samples you provide as input for this function and make a prediction based on the input features, `X_test`. It then takes the predictions and the values stored in `y_test` and runs them through the `metric` function that we created in the `criterion_factory` function. This produces a single scalar value expressing the metric.

The `classification_error` function that we used in this sample measures the difference between the real labels and predicted labels. It returns a value that expresses the percentage of samples that were incorrectly classified.

The output of the `classification_error` function should confirm what we saw when we created the confusion matrix, and will look similar to this:

```
{'metric': 0.36666666666666664, 'samples': 30}
```

The results may differ because of the random-number generator that is used to initialize the model. You can set a fixed random seed for the random-number generator using the following code:

```
import cntk
import numpy

cntk.cntk_py.set_fixed_random_seed(1337)
numpy.random.seed = 1337
```

This will fix some variances in output but not all of them. There are a few components in CNTK that ignore the fixed random seed and will still generate different results each time you run the training code.

CNTK 2.6 includes the `fmeasure` function, which implements the F-measure we discussed in the section, *Using the F-measure as an alternative to the confusion matrix*. You can use the `fmeasure` in the training code by replacing the call to `cntk.metrics.classification_error` with a call to `cntk.losses.fmeasure` when defining the `criterion factory` function:

```
import cntk

@cntk.Function
def criterion_factory(output, target):
    loss = cntk.losses.cross_entropy_with_softmax(output, target)
    metric = cntk.losses.fmeasure(output, target)
    return loss, metric
```

Running the training code again will give generate different output for the `loss.test` method call:

```
{'metric': 0.831014887491862, 'samples': 30}
```

As with the previous samples, the output may vary because of how the random-number generator is used to initialize the model.

Validating performance of a regression model

In the previous section, *Validating performance of a classification model,* we talked about validating the performance of a classification model. Now let's look at validating the performance of a regression model.

Regression models are different in that there's no binary measure of right or wrong for individual samples. Instead, you want to measure how close the prediction is to the actual value. The closer we are to the expected output, the better the model performs.

In this section, we'll discuss three methods to measure the performance of a neural network that is used for regression. We'll first talk about how to measure the performance using different error-rate functions. We'll then talk about how to use the coefficient of determination to further validate your regression model. Finally, we'll use a residual plot to get down to a very detailed level of how our model is doing.

Measuring the accuracy of your predictions

Let's first look at the basic concept of validating a regression model. As we mentioned before, you can't really say whether a prediction is right or wrong when validating a regression model. You want the prediction to be as close to the real value as possible, but a small error margin is acceptable.

You can calculate the error margin on predictions made by a regression model by looking at the distance between the predicted value and the expected value. This can be expressed as a single formula, like so:

$$error = \frac{1}{n} \sum_{i=1}^{n} (\hat{y}_i - y_i)^2$$

First, we calculate the distance between the predicted value, *y* indicated by a hat, and the real value, *y*, and square it. To get an overall error rate for the model, we'll need to sum these squared distances and calculate the average.

The square operator is needed to turn negative distances between the predicted value, y with a hat, and the real value, y, into positive distances. Without this, we would run into problems: when you have a distance of +100 and another of -100 in the next sample, you'll end up with an error rate of exactly 0. This is, of course, not what we want. The square operator solves this for us.

Because we square the distance between the prediction and actual values, we punish the computer more for large errors.

The mean squared error function can be used as a metric for validation and as a loss function during training. Mathematically, there's no difference between the two. This makes it easier to see the performance of a regression model during training. You only need to look at the loss to get an idea of the performance.

It's important to understand that you get a distance back from the mean squared error function. This is not an absolute measure of how well your model performs. You have to make a decision what maximum distance between the predicted value and expected value is acceptable to you. For example: you could specify that 90% of the predictions should have a maximum of 5% difference between the actual and the predicted value. This is very valuable for the users of your model. They typically want some form of assurance that the model predicts within certain limits.

If you're looking for performance figures that express an error margin, you're not going to find much use for the mean squared error function. Instead, you need a formula that expresses the absolute error. This can be done using the mean absolute error function:

$$error = \frac{1}{n} \sum_{i=1}^{n} |\hat{y}_i - y_i|$$

This takes the absolute distance between the predicted and the real value, sums them, and then takes the average. This will give you a number that is much more readable. For example: when you're talking about house prices, it's much more understandable to present users with a $5,000 error margin than a $25,000 squared-error margin. The latter seems rather large, but it really isn't because it is a squared value.

We're going to be purely looking at how to use the metrics from CNTK to validate a regression model. But it's good to remember to talk to the users of your model to determine what performance will be good enough.

Measuring regression model performance in CNTK

Now that we've seen how to validate regression models in theory, let's take a look at how to use the different metrics we just discussed in combination with CNTK. For this section, we'll be working with a model that predicts miles per gallon for cars using the following code:

```
from cntk import default_options, input_variable
from cntk.layers import Dense, Sequential
from cntk.ops import relu

with default_options(activation=relu):
    model = Sequential([
        Dense(64),
        Dense(64),
        Dense(1,activation=None)
    ])
features = input_variable(X.shape[1])
target = input_variable(1)

z = model(features)
```

Follow the given steps:

1. First, import the required components from the `cntk` package
2. Next, define a default activation function using the `default_options` function. We're using the `relu` function for this example
3. Create a new `Sequential` layer set and provide two `Dense` layers with `64` neurons each
4. Add an additional `Dense` layer to the `Sequential` layer set and give it `1` neuron without an activation. This layer will serve as the output layer
5. After you've created the network, create an input variable for the input features and make sure it has the same shape as the features that we're going to be using for training
6. Create another `input_variable` with size 1 to store the expected value for the neural network.

The output layer doesn't have an activation function assigned because we want it to be linear. When you leave out the activation function for a layer, CNTK will use an identity function instead and the layer will not apply a non-linearity to the data. This is useful for regression scenarios since we don't want to limit the output to a specific range of values.

To train the model, we're going to need to split the dataset and perform some preprocessing:

```
from sklearn.preprocessing import StandardScaler
from sklearn.model_selection import train_test_split

X = df_cars.drop(columns=['mpg']).values.astype(np.float32)
y = df_cars.iloc[:,0].values.reshape(-1,1).astype(np.float32)

scaler = StandardScaler()
X = scaler.fit_transform(X)

X_train, X_test, y_train, y_test = train_test_split(X, y, test_size=0.2)
```

Follow the given steps:

1. First, take the dataset and drop the mpg column using the drop method. This will produce a copy of the original dataset from which we can get the numpy vectors from the values property.
2. Next, scale the data using a StandardScaler so we get values between -1 and + 1. Doing this will help against exploding gradient problems in the neural network.
3. Finally, split the dataset into a training and validation set using the train_test_split function.

Once we have split and preprocessed the data, we can train the neural network. To train the model, we're going to define a combination of a loss and metric function to train the model:

```
import cntk

def absolute_error(output, target):
    return cntk.ops.reduce_mean(cntk.ops.abs(output - target))

@cntk.Function
def criterion_factory(output, target):
    loss = squared_error(output, target)
    metric = absolute_error(output, target)
    return loss, metric
```

Follow the given steps:

1. Define a new function named `absolute_error`
2. In the `absolute_error` function calculate the mean absolute difference between the output and target
3. Return the result
4. Next, create another function called `criterion_factory`
5. Mark this function with `@cntk.Function` to tell CNTK to include the `train` and `test` method on the function
6. Within the function, create the `loss` using the `squared_loss` function
7. Then, create the metric using the `absolute_error` function
8. Return both the `loss` and the `metric` as a tuple

CNTK will automatically combine these into a single callable function. When you invoke the `train` method, the loss is used to optimize the parameters in the neural network. When you invoke the `test` method, the metric is used to measure the performance of the previously-trained neural network.

If we want to measure the absolute error for our model we need to write our own metric, since the `mean absolute` error function isn't included in the framework. This can be done by combining the standard operators included in CNTK.

Now that we have a way to create a combined `loss` and `metric` function, let's take a look at how to use it to train the model:

```
from cntk.logging import ProgressPrinter
from cntk.losses import squared_error
from cntk.learners import sgd

loss = criterion_factory(z, target)
learner = sgd(z.parameters, 0.001)

progress_printer = ProgressPrinter(0)

train_summary = loss.train((X_train,y_train),
                           parameter_learners=[learner],
                           callbacks=[progress_printer],
                           minibatch_size=16,
                           max_epochs=10)
```

We'll use `criterion_factory` as the `loss` and `metric` combination for our model. When you train the model, you will see that the loss is going down quite nicely over time. We can also see that the mean absolute error is going down as well:

```
average       since      average      since     examples
  loss        last       metric       last

----------------------------------------------------------
Learning rate per minibatch: 0.001
   690         690         24.9        24.9          16
   654         636         24.1        23.7          48
   602         563         23.1        22.3         112
   480         373         20.4          18         240
    62          62         6.19        6.19          16
  47.6        40.4         5.55        5.24          48
  44.1        41.5         5.16        4.87         112
  32.9        23.1          4.5        3.92         240
  15.5        15.5         3.12        3.12          16
  15.7        15.7         3.13        3.14          48
  15.8        15.9         3.16        3.18         112
[...]
```

Now we need to make sure that our model handles new data just as well is it does the training data. To do this, we need to invoke the `test` method on the `loss`/`metric` combination with the test dataset:

```
loss.test((X_test,y_test))
```

This gives us the value for the performance metric and the number of samples it was run on. The output should look similar to the following. It's low and tells us that the model has a small error margin:

```
{'metric': 1.8967978561980814, 'samples': 79}
```

When we call the `test` method on the loss with the test set, it will take the test data, `X_test`, and run it through the model to obtain predictions for each of the samples. It then runs these through the `metric` function together with the expected output, `y_test`. This will result in a single scalar value as the output.

Measuring performance for out-of-memory datasets

We've talked a lot about different methods to validate the performance of your neural networks. So far, we've only had to deal with datasets that fit in memory. But this is almost never the case in production scenarios, since you need a lot of data to train a neural network. In this section, we'll discuss how to use the different metrics on out-of-memory datasets.

Measuring performance when working with minibatch sources

When you use a minibatch data source, you need a slightly different setup for the loss and metric. Let's go back and review how you can set up training using a minibatch source and extend it with metrics to validate the model. First, we need to set up a way to feed data to the trainer of the model:

```python
from cntk.io import StreamDef, StreamDefs, MinibatchSource,
CTFDeserializer, INFINITELY_REPEAT

def create_datasource(filename, limit=INFINITELY_REPEAT):
    labels_stream = StreamDef(field='labels', shape=3, is_sparse=False)
    features_stream = StreamDef(field='features', shape=4, is_sparse=False)

    deserializer = CTFDeserializer(filename,
StreamDefs(labels=labels_stream, features=features_stream))
    minibatch_source = MinibatchSource(deserializer, randomize=True,
max_sweeps=limit)
    return minibatch_source

training_source = create_datasource('iris_train.ctf')
test_source = create_datasource('iris_test.ctf', limit=1)
```

Follow the given steps:

1. First, import the components needed to create a minibatch source.
2. Next, define a new function `create_datasource` with two parameters, `filename` and `limit` with a default value of `INFINITELY_REPEAT`.
3. Within the function, create a `StreamDef` for the labels that reads from the labels field that has three features. Set the `is_sparse` keyword argument to `False`.

4. Create another `StreamDef` for the features that reads from the features field that has four features. Set the `is_sparse` keyword argument to `False`.

5. Next, initialize a new instance of `CTFDeserializer` class and specify the filename and streams that you want to deserialize.

6. Finally, Create a minibatch source using the `deserializer` and configure it to shuffle the dataset and specify the `max_sweeps` keyword argument with the configured amount of sweeps.

Remember from `Chapter 3`, *Getting Data into Your Neural Network*, that to use a minibatch source, you need to have a compatible file format. For the classification model in `Chapter 3`, *Getting Data into Your Neural Network*, we used the CTF file format as input for the MinibatchSource. We've included the data files in the sample code for this chapter. Check out the `Validating with a minibatch source.ipynb` file for more details.

Once we have the data source, we can create the model same model as we used in the earlier section, *Validating performance of a classification model*, and initialize a training session for it:

```
from cntk.logging import ProgressPrinter
from cntk.train import Trainer, training_session

minibatch_size = 16
samples_per_epoch = 150
num_epochs = 30
max_samples = samples_per_epoch * num_epochs

input_map = {
    features: training_source.streams.features,
    labels: training_source.streams.labels
}

progress_writer = ProgressPrinter(0)
trainer = Trainer(z, (loss, metric), learner, progress_writer)

session = training_session(trainer,
                           mb_source=training_source,
                           mb_size=minibatch_size,
                           model_inputs_to_streams=input_map,
                           max_samples=max_samples,
                           test_config=test_config)

session.train()
```

Follow the given steps:

1. First, import the `ProgressPrinter` to log information about the training process
2. Additionally, import the `Trainer` and `training_session` component from the `train` module
3. Next, define a mapping between the input variables of the model and the data streams from the minibatch source
4. Then, create a new instance of the `ProgressWriter` to log the output of the training progress
5. After, initialize the `trainer` and provide it with the model, the `loss`, the `metric`, the `learner` and the `progress_writer`
6. Finally, invoke the `training_session` function to start the training process. Provide the function with the `training_source`, the settings and the mapping between the input variables and the data streams from the minibatch source.

To add validation to this setup, you need to use a `TestConfig` object and assign it to the `test_config` keyword argument of the `train_session` function. The `TestConfig` object doesn't have a lot of settings that you need to configure:

```
from cntk.train import TestConfig

test_config = TestConfig(test_source)
```

Follow the given steps:

1. First, import the `TestConfig` class from the `train` module
2. Then, create a new instance of the `TestConfig` with the `test_source`, which we created earlier, as input

You can use this test configuration during training by specifying the `test_config` keyword argument for in the `train` method.

When you run the training session, you will get output that is similar to this:

average loss	since last	average metric	since last	examples
Learning rate per minibatch: 0.1				
1.57	1.57	0.214	0.214	16
1.38	1.28	0.264	0.289	48
1.41	1.44	0.147	0.0589	112
1.27	1.15	0.0988	0.0568	240
1.17	1.08	0.0807	0.0638	496

```
    1.1         1.03       0.0949      0.109           1008
    0.973       0.845      0.206       0.315           2032
    0.781       0.59       0.409       0.61            4080
Finished Evaluation [1]: Minibatch[1-1]: metric = 70.72% * 30;
```

First, you'll see that the model is trained using the data from the training MinibatchSource. Because we configured the progress printer as a callback for the training session, we can see how the loss is progressing. Additionally, you will see a metric increasing in value. This metric output comes from the fact that we gave the `training_session` function a trainer that had both a loss and a metric configured.

When the training finishes, a test pass will be performed over the model using the data coming from the MinibatchSource that you configured in the `TestConfig` object.

What's cool is that not only is your training data now loaded in memory in small batches to prevent memory issues, the test data is also loaded in small batches. This is really useful if you're working on models with large datasets, even for testing purposes.

Measuring performance when working with a manual minibatch loop

Using metrics when training with the regular APIs in CNTK is the easiest way to measure the performance of your model during and after training. Things will be more difficult when you work with a manual minibatch loop. This is the point where you get the most control though.

Let's first go back and review how to train a model using a manual minibatch loop. We're going to be working on the classification model we used in the section *Validating performance of a classification model*. You can find it in the `Validating with a manual minibatch loop.ipynb` file in the sample code for this chapter.

The loss for the model is defined as a combination of the `cross-entropy` loss function and the F-measure metric that we saw in the section *Using the F-Measure as an alternative to the confusion matrix*. You can use the function object combination that we used before in the section *Measuring classification performance in CNTK*, with a manual training process, which is a nice touch:

```
import cntk
from cntk.losses import cross_entropy_with_softmax, fmeasure

@cntk.Function
def criterion_factory(outputs, targets):
```

```
loss = cross_entropy_with_softmax(outputs, targets)
metric = fmeasure(outputs, targets, beta=1)
return loss, metric
```

Once we have a loss defined, we can use it in the trainer to set up a manual training session. As you might expect, this requires a bit more work to write it in Python code:

```python
import pandas as pd
import numpy as np
from cntk.logging import ProgressPrinter
from cntk.train import Trainer

progress_writer = ProgressPrinter(0)
trainer = Trainer(z, loss, learner, progress_writer)

for _ in range(0,30):
    input_data = pd.read_csv('iris.csv',
        names=['sepal_length', 'sepal_width','petal_length','petal_width',
'species'],
        index_col=False, chunksize=16)

    for df_batch in input_data:
        feature_values = df_batch.iloc[:,:4].values
        feature_values = feature_values.astype(np.float32)

        label_values = df_batch.iloc[:,-1]

        label_values = label_values.map(lambda x: label_mapping[x])
        label_values = label_values.values

        encoded_labels = np.zeros((label_values.shape[0], 3))
        encoded_labels[np.arange(label_values.shape[0]), label_values] = 1.

        trainer.train_minibatch({features: feature_values, labels:
encoded_labels})
```

Follow the given steps:

1. To get started, import the numpy and pandas packages to load and preprocess the data
2. Next, import the ProgressPrinter class to log information during training
3. Then, import the Trainer class from the train module
4. After importing all the necessary components, create a new instance of the ProgressPrinter
5. Then, initialize the trainer and provide it with the model, the loss, the learner and the progress_writer

6. To train the model, create a loop that iterates over the dataset thirty times. This will be our outer training loop

7. Next, load the data from disk using `pandas` and set the `chunksize` keyword argument to `16` so the dataset is loaded in mini-batches

8. Iterate over each of the mini-batches using a `for` loop, this will be our inner training loop

9. Within the `for` loop, read the first four columns using the `iloc` indexer as the `features` to train from and convert them to `float32`

10. Next, read the last column as the label to train from

11. The labels are stored as strings, but we one-hot vectors, so convert the label strings to their numeric representation

12. Then, take the numeric representation of the labels and convert them to a numpy array so its easier to work with them

13. After that, create a new numpy array that has the same number of rows as the label values that we just converted. But with 3 columns, representing the number of possible classes that the model can predict

14. Now, select the columns based on the numeric label values and set it them 1, to create one-hot encoded labels

15. Finally, invoke the `train_minibatch` method on the `trainer` and feed it the processed features and labels for the minibatch

When you run the code you swill see output similar to this:

```
average since average since   examples
loss    last   metric  last

---------------------------------------------------------
Learning rate per minibatch: 0.1
1.45    1.45   -0.189  -0.189  16
1.24    1.13   -0.0382  0.0371 48
1.13    1.04   0.141    0.276  112
1.21    1.3    0.0382  -0.0599 230
1.2     1.18   0.037    0.0358 466
```

Because we combined a metric and loss in a function object and used a progress printer in the trainer configuration, we get both the output for the loss and the metric during training.

To evaluate the model performance, you need to perform a similar task as with training the model. Only this time, we need to use an `Evaluator` instance to test the model:

```
from cntk import Evaluator

evaluator = Evaluator(loss.outputs[1], [progress_writer])
```

```
input_data = pd.read_csv('iris.csv',
        names=['sepal_length', 'sepal_width','petal_length','petal_width',
'species'],
        index_col=False, chunksize=16)

for df_batch in input_data:
    feature_values = df_batch.iloc[:,:4].values
    feature_values = feature_values.astype(np.float32)

    label_values = df_batch.iloc[:,-1]
    label_values = label_values.map(lambda x: label_mapping[x])
    label_values = label_values.values
    encoded_labels = np.zeros((label_values.shape[0], 3))
    encoded_labels[np.arange(label_values.shape[0]), label_values] = 1.
    evaluator.test_minibatch({ features: feature_values, labels:
encoded_labels})
evaluator.summarize_test_progress()
```

Follow the given steps:

1. First, import the `Evaluator` from the `cntk` package
2. Then, create a new instance of the `Evaluator` and provide it the second output of the `loss` function
3. After initializing the `Evalutator`, load the CSV file containing the data and provide the `chunksize` parameter so we load the data in batches
4. Now, iterate over the batches returned by the `read_csv` function to process the items in the dataset
5. Within this loop, read the first four columns as the `features` and convert them to `float32`
6. After that, read the labels column
7. Since the labels are stored as string we need to convert them to a numeric representation first
8. After that, take the underlying numpy array, for easier processing
9. Next, create a new array using the `np.zeros` function
10. Set the elements at the label indices we obtained in step 7 to 1 to create the one-hot encoded vectors for the labels
11. Then, invoke the `test_minibatch` method on the `evaluator` and provide it the features and encoded labels
12. Finally, use the `summarize_test_progress` method on the `evaluator` to obtain the final performance metrics

When you run the `evaluator`, you will get output similar to this:

```
Finished Evaluation [1]: Minibatch[1-11]: metric = 65.71% * 166;
```

While the manual minibatch loop is a lot more work to set up for both training and evaluation, it is one of the most powerful. You can change everything and even run evaluation at different intervals during training. This is especially useful if you have a model that takes a long time to train. By using testing at regular intervals, you can monitor when your model starts to overfit, and you can stop the training if you need to.

Monitoring your model

Now that we've done some validation on our models, it's time to talk about monitoring your model during training. You saw some of this before in the section *Measuring classification performance in CNTK* and the previous `Chapter 2`, *Building Neural Networks with CNTK*, through the use of the `ProgressWriter` class, but there are more ways to monitor your model. For example: you can use `TensorBoardProgressWriter`. Let's take a closer look at how monitoring in CNTK works and how you can use it to detect problems in your model.

Using callbacks during training and validation

CNTK allows you to specify callbacks in several spots in the API. For example: when you call train on a `loss` function, you can specify a set of callbacks through the callbacks argument:

```
train_summary = loss.train((X_train,y_train),
                           parameter_learners=[learner],
                           callbacks=[progress_writer],
                           minibatch_size=16, max_epochs=15)
```

If you're working with minibatch sources or using a manual minibatch loop, you can specify callbacks for monitoring purposes when you create the `Trainer`:

```
from cntk.logging import ProgressPrinter

callbacks = [
    ProgressPrinter(0)
]

trainer = Trainer(z, (loss, metric), learner, [callbacks])
```

CNTK will invoke these callbacks at set moments:

- When a minibatch is completed
- When a full sweep over the dataset is completed during training
- When a minibatch of testing is completed
- When a full sweep over the dataset is completed during testing

A callback in CNTK can be a callable function or a progress writer instance. The progress writers use a specific API that corresponds to the four times during which logging data is written. We'll leave the implementation of the progress writers for your own exploration. Instead, we'll look at how you can use the different progress writers during training to monitor your model.

Using ProgressPrinter

One of the monitoring tools you will find yourself using quite a lot is ProgressPrinter. This class implements basic console-based logging to monitor your model. It can also log to disk should you want it to. This is especially useful if you're working in a distributed training scenario or in a scenario where you can't log in on the console to see the output of your Python program.

You can create a ProgressPrinter instance like so:

```
ProgressPrinter(0, log_to_file='test_log.txt'),
```

You can configure quite a few things in ProgressPrinter, but we'll limit ourselves to the most-used arguments. You can, however, find more information about ProgressPrinter on the CNTK website should you want something more exotic.

When you configure ProgressPrinter, you can specify the frequency as the first argument to configure how often data should be printed to the output. When you specify a value of zero, it will print status messages every other minibatch (1,2,4,6,8,...). You can change this setting to a value greater than zero to create a custom schedule. For example, when you enter 3 as the frequency, the logger will write status data after every 3 minibatches.

The `ProgressPrinter` class also accepts a `log_to_file` argument. This is where you can specify a filename to write the log data to. The output of the file will look similar to this when used:

```
test_log.txt
CNTKCommandTrainInfo: train : 300
CNTKCommandTrainInfo: CNTKNoMoreCommands_Total : 300
CNTKCommandTrainBegin: train
 average since average since examples
    loss  last  metric  last
-------------------------------------------------------
Learning rate per minibatch: 0.1
      8.91 8.91    0.296 0.296 16
      3.64 1       0.229 0.195 48
      2.14 1.02    0.215 0.204 112
     0.875 0.875   0.341 0.341 16
     0.88 0.883    0.331 0.326 48
```

This is quite similar to what you've seen before in this chapter when we used the `ProgressPrinter` class.

Finally, you can specify how the metrics should be displayed by the `ProgressPrinter` class using the `metric_is_pct` setting. Set this to `False` to print the raw value instead of the default strategy to print the metric as a percentage.

Using TensorBoard

While `ProgressPrinter` can be useful to monitor training progress inside a Python notebook, it certainly leaves a lot to be desired. For example: getting a good view of how the loss and metric progress over time is hard with `ProgressPrinter`.

There's a great alternative to the `ProgressPrinter` class in CNTK. You can use `TensorBoardProgressWriter` to log data in a native TensorBoard format.

TensorBoard is a tool that was invented by Google to be used with TensorFlow. It can visualize all sorts of metrics from your model during and after training. You can download this tool manually by installing it using PIP:

```
pip install tensorboard
```

To use TensorBoard, you need to set up `TensorBoardProgressWriter` in your training code first:

```
import time
from cntk.logging import TensorBoardProgressWriter

tensorboard_writer =
TensorBoardProgressWriter(log_dir='logs/{}'.format(time.time()), freq=1,
model=z)
```

1. First, import the `time` package
2. Next, Import the `TensorBoardProgressWriter`
3. Finally, create a new `TensorBoardProgressWriter` and provide a timestamped directory to log to. Make sure to provide the model as a keyword argument so it gets sent to TensorBoard during training.

We opted to use a separate log `dir` for each run by parameterizing the log directory setting with a timestamp. This ensures that multiple runs on the same model are logged separately and can be viewed and compared. Finally, you can specify the model that you're using the TensorBoard progress writer with.

Once you've trained your model, make sure you call the `close` method on your `TensorboardProgressWriter` instance to ensure that the log files are fully written. Without this, you're likely to miss a few, if not all, metrics collected during training.

You can visualize the TensorBoard logging data by starting TensorBoard using the command in your Anaconda prompt:

```
tensorboard --logdir logs
```

The `--logdir` argument should match the root `dir` where all runs are logged. In this case, we're using the `logs` dir as the input source for TensorBoard. Now you can open TensorBoard in your browser by going to the URL indicated in the console where you started TensorBoard.

The TensorBoard web page looks like this, with the SCALARS tab as the default page:

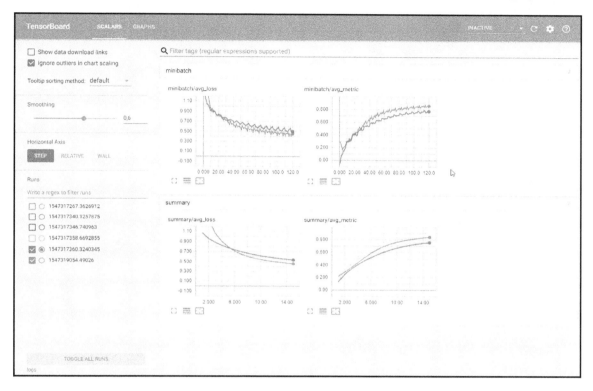

Tensorboard web page, with the scalars tab as the default page

You can view multiple runs by selecting them on the left of the screen. This allows you to compare different runs to see how much things have changed between the runs. In the middle of the screen, you can check out different charts that depict the loss and metrics over time. CNTK will log the metrics per minibatch and per epoch, and both can be used to see how metrics have changed over time.

There are more ways in which TensorBoard helps to monitor your model. When you go to the **GRAPHS** tab, you can see what your model looks like in a nice graphical map:

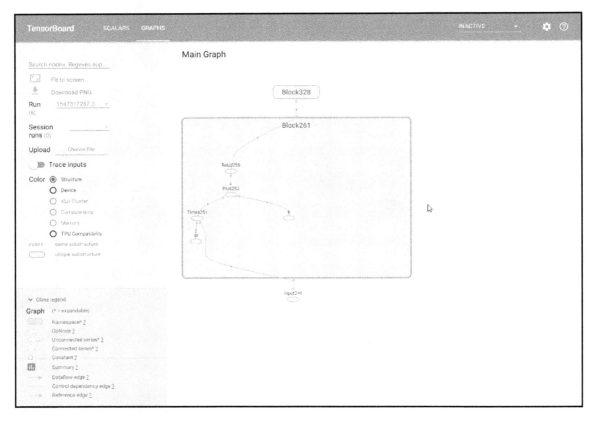

Display of your model in a graphical map

This is especially useful for technically-complex models with a lot of layers. It helps you understand how layers are connected, and it has saved many developers from a headache because they were able to find their disconnected layers through this tab.

TensorBoard contains many more ways to monitor your model, but sadly CNTK uses only the SCALARS and GRAPH tabs by default. You can also log images to TensorBoard should you work with them. We'll talk about this later in Chapter 5, *Working with Images*, when we start to work on images.

Summary

In this chapter, you learned how to validate different types of deep learning models and how you can use metrics in CNTK to implement validation logic for your models. We also explored how to use TensorBoard to visualize training progress and the structure of the model so you can easily debug your models.

Monitoring and validating your model early and often will ensure that you end up with neural networks that work very well on production and do what your client expects them to. It is the only way to detect underfitting and overfitting of your model.

Now that you know how to build and validate basic neural networks, we'll dive into more interesting deep learning scenarios. In the next chapter, we will explore how you can use images with neural networks to perform image detection, and in Chapter 6, *Working with Time Series Data*, we will take a look at how to build and validate deep learning models that work on time series data, such as financial market data. You will need all of the techniques described in this and previous chapters in the next chapters to make the most of the more advanced deep learning scenarios.

5
Working with Images

In this chapter, we're going to explore some more deep learning models with CNTK. Specifically, we're going to look at using neural networks for classifying image data. All that you've learned in the past chapters will come back in this chapter as we discuss how to train convolutional neural networks.

The following topics will be covered in this chapter:

- Convolutional neural network architecture
- How to build a convolutional neural network
- How to feed image data into a convolutional network
- How to improve network performance with data augmentation

Technical requirements

We assume you have a recent version of Anaconda installed on your computer and have followed the steps in Chapter 1, *Getting Started with CNTK*, to install CNTK on your computer. The sample code for this chapter can be found in our GitHub repository at: https://github.com/PacktPublishing/Deep-Learning-with-Microsoft-Cognitive-Toolkit-Quick-Start-Guide/tree/master/ch5.

In this chapter, we'll work on an example stored in a Jupyter notebook. To access the sample code, run the following commands inside an Anaconda prompt in the directory where you've downloaded the code:

```
cd ch5
jupyter notebook
```

We'll mention relevant notebooks in each of the sections so you can follow along and try out the different techniques yourself.

The dataset for this chapter is not available in the GitHub repository. It would be too big to store there. Please open the `Prepare the dataset.ipynb` notebook and follow the instructions there to obtain the data for this chapter.

Check out the following video to see the code in action:

`http://bit.ly/2Wm6U49`

Convolutional neural network architecture

In previous chapters, we've learned how to use regular feed-forward network architectures to build neural networks. In a feed-forward neural network, we assume that there are interactions between the different input features. But we don't make any assumptions about the nature of these interactions. This is, however, not always the right thing to do.

When you work with complex data such as images, a feed-forward neural network won't do a very good job. This comes from the fact that we assume that there's an interaction between the inputs of our network. But we don't account for the fact that they are organized in a spatial way. When you look at the pixels in an image, there's a horizontal and vertical relationship between them. There's also a relationship between the colors in an image and the position of certain colored pixels in that image.

A convolutional network is a special kind of neural network that makes the explicit assumption that we're dealing with data that has a spatial relationship to it. This makes it really good at recognizing images. But other spatially organized data will work too. Let's explore the architecture of a convolutional neural network used for image classification tasks.

Network architecture used for image classification

Convolutional networks used for image classification typically contain one or more convolution layers followed by pooling layers, and usually end in regular fully-connected layers to provide the final output as shown in the following screenshot:

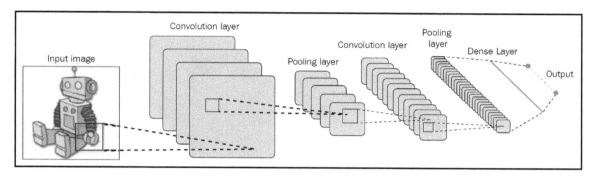

This image is from: https://en.wikipedia.org/wiki/File:Typical_cnn.png

When you take a closer look at the structure of a convolutional network, you'll see that it starts with a set of **convolution** and **pooling** layers. You can consider this part a complex, trainable photo filter. The **convolution layers** filter out interesting details that are needed to classify the image, and the **pooling layers** summarize these features so that there are fewer data points to crunch near the end of the network.

Usually, you will find several sets of convolution layers and pooling layers in a neural network for image classification. This is done to be able to extract more complex details from the image. The first layer of the network extracts simple details, such as lines, from the image. The next set of layers then combines the output of the previous set of layers to learn more complex features, such as corners or curves. As you can imagine, the layers after that are used to learn increasingly more complex features.

Often, when you build a neural network, you want to classify what's in the image. This is where the classic dense layers play an important role. Typically, a model used for image recognition will end in one output layer and one or more dense layers.

Let's take a look at how to work with convolutional and pooling layers to create a convolutional neural network.

Working with convolution layers

Now that you've seen what a convolutional network looks like, let's look at the convolution layer that is used in the convolutional network:

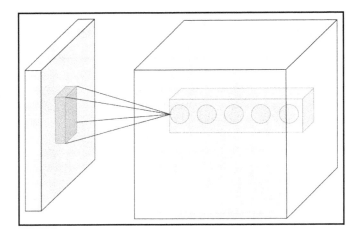

This image is from: https://en.wikipedia.org/wiki/File:Conv_layer.png

The convolution layer is the core building block of the convolutional network. You can consider the convolution layer a trainable filter that you can use to extract important details from the input and remove data that is considered noise. A convolution layer contains a set of weights that cover a small area (width and height) but cover all channels of the input given to the layer. When you create a convolution layer, you need to specify its depth in neurons. You'll find that most frameworks, including CNTK, talk about filters when talking about the depth of the layer.

When we perform a forward pass, we slide the filters of the layer across the input and perform a dot product operation between the input and the weights for each of the filters. The sliding motion is controlled by a stride setting. When you specify a stride of 1, you will end up with an output matrix that has the same width and height as the input, but with the same depth as the number of filters in the layer. You can set a different stride, which will reduce the width and height of the output matrix.

In addition to the input size and number of filters, you can configure the padding of the layer. Adding padding to a convolution layer will add a border of zeros around the processed input data. This may sound like a weird thing to do but can come in quite handy in some situations.

When you look at the output size of a convolution layer, it will be determined based on the input size, the number of filters, the stride, and padding. The formula looks like this:

$$Output = \frac{W - F - 2P}{S} + 1$$

W is the input size, *F* is the number of filters or depth of the layer, *P* the padding, and *S* the stride.

Not all combinations of input size, filters, stride, and padding are valid, though. For example, when you have an input size *W* = 10 and a layer depth *F* = 3 and a stride *S* = 2, then you'll end up with an output volume of 5.5. Not all inputs will perfectly map to this output size, so CNTK will raise an exception. This is where the padding setting comes in. By specifying padding, we can make sure that all inputs are mapped to output neurons.

The settings for input size and filters we've just discussed may feel a little abstract, but there's sense to them. Setting a larger input size will cause the layer to capture coarser patterns from the input. Setting a smaller input size will make the layer better at detecting finer patterns. The depth or number of filters controls how many different patterns can be detected in the input image. At a high level, you could say that a convolutional filter with one filter detects one pattern; for example, horizontal lines. A layer with two filters can detect two different patterns: horizontal and vertical lines.

Coming up with the right settings for a convolutional network can be quite a bit of work. Luckily, CNTK has settings that help make this process a little less complex.

Training a convolutional layer is done in the same way as a regular dense layer. This means that we'll perform a forward pass, calculate the gradients, and use the learner to come up with better values for the parameters in a backward pass.

Convolution layers are often followed by a pooling layer to compress the features learned by the convolutional layer. Let's look at pooling layers next.

Working with pooling layers

In the previous section we've looked at convolutional layers and how they can be used to extract details from pixel data. Pooling layers are used to summarize the extracted details. Pooling layers help reduce the volume of data so that it becomes easier to classify this data.

It's important to understand that neural networks have a harder time to classify a sample when the sample has a lot of different input features. That's why we use a combination of convolution layers and pooling layers to extract details and summarize them:

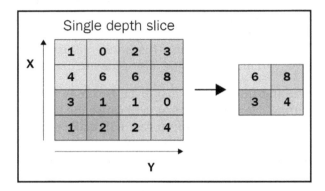

This image is from: https://en.wikipedia.org/wiki/File:Max_pooling.png

A pooling layer features a downsampling algorithm that you configure with an input size and stride. We will feed the output of each filter in the previous convolution layer into the pooling layer. The pooling layer moves across the slices of data and takes small windows equal to the configured input size. It takes the small areas of values and grabs the highest value from them as the output for that area. Just like with the convolution layer, it uses the stride to control how fast it moves across the input. For example, a size of 1 combined with a stride of 2 will reduce the data dimensions by half. By using only the highest input value, it discards 75% of the input data.

Max-sampling, as this pooling technique is called, is not the only way in which a pooling layer can reduce the dimensionality of the input data. You can also use average-pooling. In this case, the average value of the input area is used as output in the pooling layer.

Note that pooling layers only reduce the size of the input along the width and height. The depth remains the same as before, so you can rest assured that features are only downsampled and not removed completely.

Since pooling layers have a fixed algorithm to downsample input data, there are no trainable parameters in them. This means that it takes no time to train pooling layers.

Other uses for convolutional networks

We're focusing our efforts on using convolutional networks for image classification, but you can use this kind of neural network for many more scenarios, for example:

- Object detection in images. The CNTK website includes a nice example that shows how to build an object detection model: https://docs.microsoft.com/en-us/cognitive-toolkit/Object-Detection-using-Fast-R-CNN
- Detect faces in photos and predict the age of the person in the photo
- Caption images using a combination of convolutional and recurrent neural networks that we discuss in Chapter 6, *Working with Time Series Data*
- Predict the distance to the bottom of a lake from sonar images

When you start to combine convolutional networks for different tasks, you can build some pretty powerful applications; for example, a security camera that detects people in the videostream and warns the security guard about trespassers.

Countries such as China are investing heavily in this kind of technology. Convolutional networks are used in smart city applications to monitor crossings. Using a deep learning model, the authorities can detect accidents at traffic lights and reroute the traffic automatically so that the police have an easier job.

Building convolutional networks

Now that you've seen the basics behind convolutional networks and some common use cases for them, let's take a look at how to build one with CNTK.

We're going to build a model that can recognize handwritten digits in images. There's a free dataset available called the MNIST dataset that contains 60,000 samples of handwritten digits. There's also a test set available with 10,000 samples for the MNIST dataset.

Let's get started and see what building a convolutional network looks like in CNTK. First, we'll look at how to put together the structure of the convolutional neural network, we then will take a look at how to train the parameters of a convolutional neural network. Finally, we'll explore how to improve the neural network by changing it's structure with different layer setups.

Building the network structure

Typically, when you build a neural network for recognizing patterns in images, you will use a combination of convolution and pooling layers. The end of the network should contain one or more hidden layers, ending with a softmax layer for classification purposes.

Let's build the network structure:

```
from cntk.layers import Convolution2D, Sequential, Dense, MaxPooling
from cntk.ops import log_softmax, relu
from cntk.initializer import glorot_uniform
from cntk import input_variable, default_options

features = input_variable((3,28,28))
labels = input_variable(10)

with default_options(initialization=glorot_uniform, activation=relu):
    model = Sequential([
        Convolution2D(filter_shape=(5,5), strides=(1,1), num_filters=8,
pad=True),
        MaxPooling(filter_shape=(2,2), strides=(2,2)),
        Convolution2D(filter_shape=(5,5), strides=(1,1), num_filters=16,
pad=True),
        MaxPooling(filter_shape=(3,3), strides=(3,3)),
        Dense(10, activation=log_softmax)
    ])

z = model(features)
```

Follow the given steps:

1. First, import the required layers for the neural network.
2. Then, import the activation functions for the network.
3. Next, import the `glorot_uniform initializer` function to initialize the convolutional layers later.
4. After that, import the `input_variable` function to create input variables and the `default_options` function to make configuration of the neural network a little easier.
5. Create a new `input_variable` store the input images, they will contain 3 channels (red, green, and blue) and have a size of 28 by 28 pixels.
6. Create another `input_variable` to store the labels to predict.
7. Next, create the `default_options` for the network and use the `glorot_uniform` as the initialization function.

8. Then, create a new `Sequential` layer set to structure the neural network

9. Within the `Sequential` layer set, add a `Convolutional2D` layer with a `filter_shape` of 5 and a `strides` setting of 1 and set the number of filters to 8. Enable `padding` so the image is padded to retain the original dimensions.

10. Add a `MaxPooling` layer with a `filter_shape` of 2 and a `strides` setting of 2 to compress the image by half.

11. Add another `Convolution2D` layer with a `filter_shape` of 5 and a `strides` setting of 1, use 16 filters. Add `padding` to retain the size of the image produced by the previous pooling layer.

12. Next, add another `MaxPooling` layer with a `filter_shape` of 3 and a `strides` setting of 3 to reduce the image to a third.

13. Finally, add a `Dense` layer with 10 neurons for the 10 possible classes the network can predict. Use a `log_softmax` activation function to turn the network into a classification model.

We're using images of 28x28 pixels as the input for the model. This size is fixed, so when you want to make a prediction with this model, you need to provide the same size images as input.

 Note that this model is still very basic and will not produce perfect results, but it is a good start. Later on, we can start to tune it should we need to.

Training the network with images

Now that we have the structure of the convolutional neural network, let's explore how to train it. Training a neural network that works with images requires more memory than most computers have available. This is where the minibatch sources from Chapter 3, *Getting Data into Your Neural Network*, come into play. We're going to set up a set of two minibatch sources to train and evaluate the neural network we've just created. Let's first take a look at how to construct a minibatch source for images:

```
import os
from cntk.io import MinibatchSource, StreamDef, StreamDefs,
ImageDeserializer, INFINITELY_REPEAT
import cntk.io.transforms as xforms

def create_datasource(folder, max_sweeps=INFINITELY_REPEAT):
    mapping_file = os.path.join(folder, 'mapping.bin')
    stream_definitions = StreamDefs(
```

```
        features=StreamDef(field='image', transforms=[]),
        labels=StreamDef(field='label', shape=10)
    )
    deserializer = ImageDeserializer(mapping_file, stream_definitions)
    return MinibatchSource(deserializer, max_sweeps=max_sweeps)
```

Follow the given steps:

1. First, Import the `os` package to get access to some useful filesystem functions.
2. Next, import the necessary components to create a new `MinibatchSource`.
3. Create a new function `create_datasource` which takes the path to an input folder and a `max_sweeps` setting to control how often we can iterate over the dataset.
4. Within the `create_datasource` function, locate the mapping.bin file within the source folder. This file will contain a mapping between the image on disk and its associated label.
5. Then create a set of stream definitions to read from the mapping.bin file.
6. Add a `StreamDef` for the image file. Make sure to include the `transforms` keyword argument and initialize it with an empty array.
7. Add another `StreamDef` for the labels field with 10 features.
8. Create a new `ImageDeserializer` and provide it the `mapping_file` and the `stream_definitions` variables.
9. Finally, create a `MinibatchSource` and provide it with the deserializer and the `max_sweeps` setting.

Note, you can create the files necessary for training using the code in the `Preparing the dataset.ipynb` Python notebook. Make sure you have enough room on your hard drive to store the images. 1 GB of hard drive space is enough to store all samples for training and validation.

Once we have the `create_datasource` function, we can create two separate data sources to train the model:

```
train_datasource = create_datasource('mnist_train')
test_datasource = create_datasource('mnist_test', max_sweeps=1,
train=False)
```

1. First, call the `create_datasource` function with the `mnist_train` folder to create the data source for training.
2. Next, call the `create_datasource` function with the `mnist_test` folder and set the `max_sweeps` to 1 to create the datasource for validating the neural network.

Once you've prepared the images, it's time to start training the neural network. We can use the `train` method on the `loss` function to kick off the training process:

```
from cntk import Function
from cntk.losses import cross_entropy_with_softmax
from cntk.metrics import classification_error
from cntk.learners import sgd

@Function
def criterion_factory(output, targets):
    loss = cross_entropy_with_softmax(output, targets)
    metric = classification_error(output, targets)
    return loss, metric

loss = criterion_factory(z, labels)
learner = sgd(z.parameters, lr=0.2)
```

Follow the given steps:

1. First, import the Function decorator from the cntk package.
2. Next, import the `cross_entropy_with_softmax` function from the losses module.
3. Then, import the `classification_error` function from the metrics module.
4. After that, import the `sgd` learner from the learners module.
5. Create a new function `criterion_factory` with two parameters, output and targets.
6. Mark the function with the `@Function` decorator to turn it into a CNTK function object.
7. Within the function, create a new instance of the `cross_entropy_with_softmax` function.
8. Next, create a new instance of the `classification_error` metric.
9. Return both the loss and metric as a result of the function.
10. After creating the `criterion_factory` function, initialize a new loss with it.
11. Finally, setup the `sgd` learner with the parameters of the model and a learning rate of 0.2.

Now that we've setup the loss and learner for the neural network, let's look at how to train and validate the neural network:

```
from cntk.logging import ProgressPrinter
from cntk.train import TestConfig

progress_writer = ProgressPrinter(0)
```

```
test_config = TestConfig(test_datasource)

input_map = {
    features: train_datasource.streams.features,
    labels: train_datasource.streams.labels
}

loss.train(train_datasource,
           max_epochs=1,
           minibatch_size=64,
           epoch_size=60000,
           parameter_learners=[learner],
           model_inputs_to_streams=input_map,
           callbacks=[progress_writer, test_config])
```

Follow the given steps:

1. First import the `ProgressPrinter` class from the `logging` module
2. Next, import the `TestConfig` class from the `train` module.
3. Create a new instance of the `ProgressPrinter` so we can log the output of the training process.
4. Then, create the `TestConfig` for the neural network using the `test_datasource` that we made earlier as input.
5. Create a new dictionary to map the data streams from the `train_datasource` to the input variables of the neural network.
6. Finally, call the `train` method on the `loss` and provide the `train_datasource`, the settings for the trainer, the `learner`, `input_map` and callbacks to use during training.

When you execute the python code, you will get back output that looks similar to this:

average loss	since last	average metric	since last	examples
Learning rate per minibatch: 0.2				
105	105	0.938	0.938	64
1.01e+07	1.51e+07	0.901	0.883	192
4.31e+06	2	0.897	0.895	448
2.01e+06	2	0.902	0.906	960
9.73e+05	2	0.897	0.893	1984
4.79e+05	2	0.894	0.891	4032
[...]				

Notice how the loss decreases over time. It does take quite a long time to reach a low enough value for the model to be usable. Training an image classification model will take a very long time, so this is one of the cases where using GPU will make a big difference to the amount of time it takes to train the model.

Picking the right combination of layers

In previous sections we've seen how to use convolutional and pooling layers to build a neural network.

We've just seen that it takes quite a long time to train a model used for image recognition. Aside from the long training time, picking the right setup for a convolutional network is very hard and takes a long time. Often you will need hours of running experiments to find a network structure that works. This can be very demotivating for aspiring AI developers.

Lucky for us, there are several research groups working on finding the best architecture for neural networks used in image classification tasks. There are several different architectures that have been used successfully in competitions and real-life scenarios:

- VGG-16
- ResNet
- Inception

And there are several more. While we can't go into detail on how to build each of these architectures work, let's explore them on a functional level to see how they work so that you can make a more informed choice about which network architecture to try in your own application.

The VGG network architecture was invented by the Visual Geometry Group as a way to classify images in 1,000 different categories. This is quite hard to do, but the team managed to get an accuracy of 70.1%, which is quite good, considering how hard it is to differentiate between 1,000 different categories

The VGG network architecture uses stacks of convolution layers with an input size of 3x3. The layers get an ever-increasing depth. Starting at layers with 32 filters, continuing with 48 filters, all the way up to 512 filters. The reduction of the data volume is done using 2x2 pooling filters. The VGG network architecture was state-of-the-art when it was invented in 2015, as it had much better accuracy than the models invented previously.

There are other ways to build neural networks for image recognition, though. The ResNet architecture uses what's called a micro-architecture. It still uses convolution layers, but this time they are arranged in blocks. The architecture is still very similar to other convolutional networks, but where the VGG network has long chain layers, the ResNet architecture has skip connections around blocks of convolution layers:

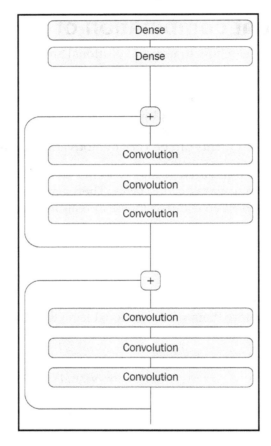

ResNet architecture

This is where the term micro-architecture comes from. Each of the blocks is a micro-network capable of learning patterns from the input. Each block has several convolution layers and a residual connection. This connection bypasses the block of convolution layers, and the data coming from this residual connection is added to the output of the convolution layers. The idea behind this is that the residual connection shakes up the learning process in the network so that it learns better and faster.

Compared to the VGG network architecture, the ResNet architecture is deeper but easier to train since it has fewer parameters that you need to optimize. The VGG network architecture takes up 599 MB of memory, while the ResNet architecture takes only 102 MB.

The final network architecture that we'll explore is the Inception architecture. This architecture is also one from the micro-architecture category. Instead of the residual blocks that are used in the ResNet architecture, the inception network uses inception blocks:

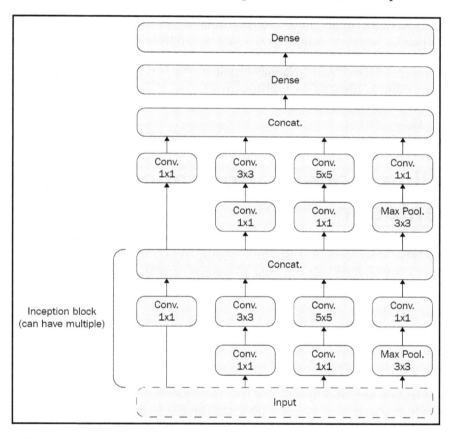

Inception Network

The inception blocks in the Inception architecture use convolution layers with different input sizes of 1x1, 3x3, and 5x5, which are then concatenated along the channel axis. This generates a matrix that has the same width and height as the input but has more channels than the input. The idea is that when you do this, you have a much better spread of features extracted from the input and thus much better quality data to perform the classification task on. The Inception architecture depicted here is very shallow; the full version used normally can have more than two inception blocks.

When you start to work on the other convolutional network architectures you will quickly find that you need a lot more computational power to train them. Often, the dataset won't fit into memory and your computer will just be too slow to train the model within a reasonable amount of time. This is where distributed training can help out. If you're interested in training models using multiple machines, you should definitely take a look at this chapter in the CNTK manual: `https://docs.microsoft.com/en-us/cognitive-toolkit/Multiple-GPUs-and-machines`.

Improving model performance with data augmentation

Neural networks used for image recognition not only are difficult to set up and train, they also require a lot of data to train. Also, they tend to overfit on the images used during training. For example, when you only use photos of faces in an upright position, your model will have a hard time recognizing faces that are rotated in another direction.

To help overcome problems with rotation and shifts in certain directions, you can use image augmentation. CNTK supports specific transforms when creating a minibatch source for images.

We've included an additional notebook for this chapter that demonstrates how to use the transformations. You can find the sample code for this section in the `Recognizing hand-written digits with augmented data.ipynb` file in the samples for this chapter.

There are several transformations that you can use. For example, you can randomly crop images used for training with just a few lines of code. Other transformations you can use are scale and color. You can find more information about these transformations on the CNTK website: `https://cntk.ai/pythondocs/cntk.io.transforms.html`.

Within the function used to create the minibatch source earlier in this chapter, we can change the list of transforms by including a cropping transform as shown in the following code:

```
import os
from cntk.io import MinibatchSource, StreamDef, StreamDefs,
ImageDeserializer, INFINITELY_REPEAT
import cntk.io.transforms as xforms

def create_datasource(folder, train=True, max_sweeps=INFINITELY_REPEAT):
    mapping_file = os.path.join(folder, 'mapping.bin')
    image_transforms = []
    if train:
        image_transforms += [
            xforms.crop(crop_type='randomside', side_ratio=0.8),
            xforms.scale(width=28, height=28, channels=3,
interpolations='linear')
        ]
    stream_definitions = StreamDefs(
        features=StreamDef(field='image', transforms=image_transforms),
        labels=StreamDef(field='label', shape=10)
    )
    deserializer = ImageDeserializer(mapping_file, stream_definitions)
    return MinibatchSource(deserializer, max_sweeps=max_sweeps)
```

We've enhanced the function to include a set of image transforms. When we're training, we will randomly crop the image so we get more variations of the image. This changes the dimensions of the image, however, so we need to also include a scale transformation to make sure that it fits the size expected by the input layer of our neural network.

Using these transforms during training will increase the variation in the training data, which reduces the chance that your neural network gets stuck on images that have a slightly different color, rotation, or size.

Be aware, though, that these transforms don't generate new samples. They simply change the data before it is fed into the trainer. You will want to increase the maximum number of epochs to allow for enough random samples to be generated with these transforms applied. How many extra epochs of training you need will depend on the size of your dataset.

It's also important to keep in mind that the dimensions of the input layer and intermediate layers have a large impact on the capabilities of the convolutional network. Larger images will naturally work better when you want to detect small objects. Scaling images back to a much smaller size will make the smaller object disappear or lose too much detail to be recognizable by the network.

Convolutional networks that support larger images will, however, take a lot more computation power to optimize, so it will take longer to train them and it will be harder to get optimal results.

Ultimately, you will need to balance a combination of image size, layer dimensions, and what data augmentation you use to get optimal results.

Summary

In this chapter, we've looked at using neural networks to classify images. It's very different from working with normal data. Not only do we need a lot more training data to get the right result, we also need a different architecture to work with images that is better suited for the job.

We've seen how convolution layers and pooling layers can be used to essentially create an advanced photo filter that extracts important details from the data and summarize these details to reduce the dimensionality of the input to a manageable size.

Once we have used the advanced properties of the convolution filters and pooling filters, it's back to business as usual with dense layers to produce a classification network.

It can be quite hard to come up with a good structure for an image classification model, so it's always a good idea to check out one of the existing architectures before venturing into image classification. Also, using the right kind of augmentation techniques can help quite a bit to get better performance.

Working with images is just one of the scenarios where deep learning is powerful. In the next chapter, we'll look at how to use deep learning to train models on time-series data, such as stock exchange information, or course information for things such as Bitcoin. We'll learn how to use sequences in CNTK and how to build a neural network that can reason over time. See you in the next chapter.

Working with Time Series Data 6

Classifying images with a neural network is one of the most iconic jobs in deep learning. But it certainly isn't the only job that neural networks excel at. Another area where there's a lot of research happening is recurrent neural networks.

In this chapter, we'll dive into recurrent neural networks, and how they can be used in scenarios where you have to deal with time series data; for example, in an IoT solution where you need to predict temperatures or other important values.

The following topics are covered in this chapter:

- What are recurrent neural networks?
- Usage scenarios for recurrent neural networks
- How do recurrent neural networks work
- Building recurrent neural networks with CNTK

Technical requirements

We assume that you have a recent version of Anaconda installed on your computer, and have followed the steps in Chapter 1, *Getting Started with CNTK*, to install CNTK on your computer. The sample code for this chapter can be found in our GitHub repository at https://github.com/PacktPublishing/Deep-Learning-with-Microsoft-Cognitive-Toolkit-Quick-Start-Guide/tree/master/ch6.

In this chapter, we'll work on an example stored in Jupyter notebooks. To access the sample code, run the following commands inside an Anaconda prompt in the directory where you've downloaded the code:

```
cd ch6
jupyter notebook
```

The sample code is stored in the `Training recurrent neural networks.ipynb` notebook. Please be aware that running the sample code for this chapter will take a long time if you don't have a machine with a GPU that can be used by CNTK.

Check out the following video to see the Code in Action:
http://bit.ly/2TAdtyr

What are recurrent neural networks?

Recurrent neural networks are a special breed of neural networks that are capable of reasoning over time. They are primarily used in scenarios where you have to deal with values that change over time.

In a regular neural network, you can provide only one input, which results in one prediction. This limits what you can do with a regular neural network. For example, regular neural networks are not good at translating text, while there have been quite a few successful experiments with recurrent neural networks in translation tasks.

In a recurrent neural network, it is possible to provide a sequence of samples that result in a single prediction. You can also use a recurrent neural network to predict an output sequence based on a single input sample. Finally, you can predict an output sequence based on an input sequence.

As with the other types of neural networks, you can use recurrent neural networks in classification jobs as well as regression tasks, although it may be harder to recognize the kind of job performed with a recurrent network based on the output of the network.

Recurrent neural networks variations

Recurrent neural networks can be used in a variety of ways. In this section we'll take a look at the different variations of recurrent neural networks and how they can be used to solve specific types of problems. Specifically we'll look at the following variations:

- Predicting a single output based on an input sequence
- Predicting a sequence based on a single input value
- Predicting sequences based on other sequences

Finally we'll also explore stacking multiple recurrent neural networks together and how that helps get better performance in a scenario like processing text.

Let's take a look at the scenarios in which recurrent networks can be used, as there are several ways in which you can use the unique properties of recurrent neural networks.

Predicting a single output based on a sequence

A recurrent neural network contains a loopback connection to the input. When we feed a sequence of values it will process each element in the sequence as time steps. Because of the loopback connection it can combine output generated when processing one element in the sequence with input for the next element in the sequence. By combining the output of previous time steps with the input of the next time steps it will build a memory over the whole sequence which can be used to make a prediction. Schematically, a basic recurrent neural network looks like this:

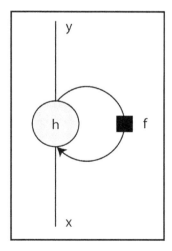

This recurrent behavior becomes clearer when we unroll a recurrent neural network into its individual steps, as demonstrated in the following diagram:

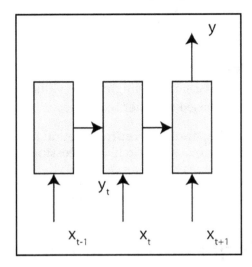

To make a prediction with this recurrent neural network we'll perform the following steps:

1. First, we feed the first element of the input sequence to create an initial hidden state.
2. Then, we take the initial hidden state and combine it with the second element in the input sequence to produce an updated hidden state.
3. Finally, we take the third element in the input sequence to produce the final hidden state and predict the output for the recurrent neural network.

Because of this loopback connection, you can teach a recurrent neural network to recognize patterns that happen over time. For example, when you want to predict tomorrow's temperature, you will need to look at the weather from the past few days to discover a pattern that can be used to determine the temperature for tomorrow.

Predicting a sequence based on a single sample

The basic model for a recurrent neural network can be extended to other use cases as well. For example, you can use the same network architecture to predict a sequence of values based on a single input as is shown in the next diagram:

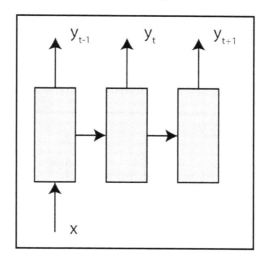

In this scenario we have three time steps, each time step will predict one step in the output sequence based on the input we provided.

1. First, we feed an input sample into the neural network to produce the initial hidden state and predict the first element in the output sequence
2. Then, we combine the initial hidden state with the same sample to produce an updated hidden state and output for the second element in the output sequence
3. Finally, we feed the sample another time to update the hidden state one more time and predict the final element in the output sequence

Generating a sequence from one sample is very different from our previous sample where we collected information about all time steps in the input sequence to get a single prediction. In this scenario we generate output at each time step.

There's one more variation on the recurrent neural network that takes concepts of the setup we just discussed with the setup that we discussed in the previous section to predict a sequence of values based on a sequence of values.

Predicting sequences based on sequences

Now that we've seen how to predict a single value based on a sequence and predicting a sequence based on a single value, let's take a look at predicting sequences for sequences. In this scenario, you perform the same steps as in the previous scenario, where we predicted a sequence based on a single sample, as is demonstrated in the following diagram:

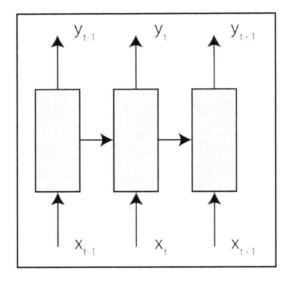

In this scenario we have three time steps that take in elements from the input sequence and predict a corresponding element in the output sequence that we want to predict. Let's go over the scenario step-by-step:

1. First, we take the first element in the input sequence and create an initial hidden state and predict the first element in the output sequence.
2. Next, we take the initial hidden state and the second element from the input sequence to update the hidden state and predict the second element in the output sequence.
3. Finally, we take the updated hidden state and the final element in the input sequence to predict the final element in the output sequence.

So Instead of repeating the same input sample for each step, like we did in the previous section, we feed in the input sequence one element at a time, and keep the generated prediction of each step as the output sequence of the model.

Stacking multiple recurrent layers

Recurrent neural networks can have multiple recurrent layers. This makes the memory capacity of the recurrent network bigger, enabling the model to learn more complex relations.

For example, when you want to translate text, you need to stack together at least two recurrent layers, one to encode the input text to an intermediate form, and another one to decode it in to the language into which you want to translate the text. Google has an interesting paper that demonstrates how to use this technique to translate from one language to another that is available at `https://arxiv.org/abs/1409.3215`.

Because you can use a recurrent neural network in so many ways, it is quite versatile in making predictions with time series data. In the next section, we'll dive into more detail of how a recurrent network works internally, to get a good grasp of how the hidden state works.

How do recurrent neural networks work?

In order to understand how recurrent neural networks work, we need to take a closer look at how recurrent layers in these networks work. There are several different types of recurrent layers you can use in a recurrent neural network. Before we dive into the more advanced versions of recurrent units, let's first discuss how to predict output with a standard recurrent layer, and how to train a neural network that contains recurrent layers.

Making predictions with a recurrent neural network

A basic recurrent layer is quite different from a regular layer in a neural network. Recurrent layers, in general, feature a hidden state that serves as the memory for the layer. There's a loopback connection from the output of the layer back to the input of the layer, as demonstrated in the following diagram:

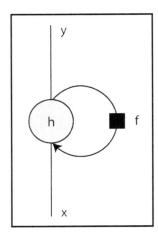

Now that we've seen what a basic recurrent layer looks like, let's go over how this layer type works step-by-step, using a sequence of three elements. Each step in the sequence is called a time step. To predict output with a recurrent layer, we need to initialize the layer with an initial hidden state. This is usually done using all zeros. The hidden state has the same size as the number of features in a single time step in the input sequence.

Next, we will need to update the hidden state for the first time step in the sequence. To update the hidden state for the first time step we'll use the following formula:

$$h_t = tanh(W_{hh} h_{initial} + W_{xh} x_t)$$

In this formula we calculate the new hidden state by calculating the dot product (that is, the element-wise product) between the initial hidden state (initialized with zeros) and a set of weights. We'll add to this the dot product between another set of weights and the input for the layer. The result of the sum of both dot products is passed through an activation function, just like in a regular neural network layer. This gives us the hidden state for the current time step.

The hidden state for the current time step is used as the initial hidden state for the next time step in the sequence. We'll repeat the calculations performed in the first time step to update the hidden state for the second time step. The formula for the second time step is shown below:

$$h_{t+1} = tanh(W_{hh}h_t + W_{xh}x_{t+1})$$

We'll calculate the dot product between the weights for the hidden state, and the hidden state from step 1, and add to this the dot product between the input and the weights for the input. Note that we're reusing the weights from the previous time step.

We'll repeat the process of updating the hidden state for the third and final step in the sequence, as shown in the following formula:

$$h_{t+2} = tanh(W_{hh}h_{t+1} + W_{xh}xt + 2)$$

When we've processed all the steps in the sequence we can calculate the output using a third set of weights and the hidden state from the final time step, as shown in the following formula:

$$y = W_{hy}h_{t+2}$$

When you're using a recurrent network to predict an output sequence, you will need to perform this final calculation at every time step, instead of just the final time step in the sequence.

Training a recurrent neural network

As with regular neural network layers, you can train a recurrent layer using backpropagation. This time, we're going to apply a trick to the regular backpropagation algorithm.

In a regular neural network, you'd calculate the gradients based on the `loss` function, the input, and the expected output of the model. But this won't work for a recurrent neural network. The loss of a recurrent layer can't be calculated using a single sample, the target value, and the `loss` function. Because the predicted output is based on all time steps in the input of the network, you also need to calculate the loss using all time steps of the input sequence. So, instead of a single set of gradients, you get a sequence of gradients that results in the final loss when summed up.

Backpropagation over time is harder than regular backpropagation. To reach the global optimum for a `loss` function, we need to work harder to descend down the gradients. The hillside for our gradient descent algorithm to walk down is much higher than with a regular neural network. Aside from higher losses, it also takes longer because we need to process each time step in the sequence to calculate and optimize the loss for a single input sequence.

To make things worse, there's a bigger chance we will see exploding gradients during backpropagation, because of the addition of gradients over multiple time steps. You can resolve the problem with exploding gradients by using a bounded activation, such as the **hyperbolic tangent function (tanh)** or `sigmoid`. These activation functions limit the output value of the recurrent layer to values between -1 and 1 for the `tanh` function, and 0 and 1 for the `sigmoid` function. The `ReLU` activation function is less useful in a recurrent neural network, because the gradients are not limited, which will definitely lead to exploding gradients at some point.

Limiting the values produced by the activation function can cause another problem. Remember from `Chapter 2`, *Building Neural Networks with CNTK*, that the `sigmoid` has a specific curve where the gradients quickly decrease to zero at both ends of the curve. The `tanh` function that we've been using in the sample in this section has the same type of curve, as demonstrated in the following diagram:

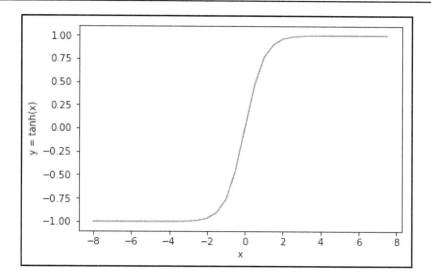

Input values between -2 and +2 have a reasonably well-defined gradient. This means that we can effectively use gradient descent to optimize the weights in the neural network. However, when the output of the recurrent layer gets lower than -2 or higher than +2, the gradient gets shallower. This can get extremely low, to a point where the CPU or GPU starts to round the gradients to zero. This means that we are no longer learning.

Recurrent layers suffer more from the vanishing gradient or saturation problem than regular neural network layers because of the multiple time steps involved. You can't do much about it when using a regular recurrent layer. There are, however, other recurrent layer types that have a more advanced setup that can solve this problem to some extent.

Using other recurrent layer types

Because of the vanishing gradient problem, the basic recurrent layer is not very good at learning long-term correlations. In other words, it does not handle long sequences very well. You run in into this problem when you try to process sentences or longer sequences of text and try to classify what they mean. In English and other languages, there's quite a long distance between two related words in a sentence that give the sentence meaning. When you only use a basic recurrent layer in your model, you will quickly discover that your model won't be very good at classifying sequences of text.

There are, however, other recurrent layer types that are much more suited for working with longer sequences. Also, they tend to combine long and short-term correlations better.

Working with gated recurrent units

One alternative to the basic recurrent layer is the **Gated Recurrent Unit (GRU)**. This layer type has two gates that help it handle long-distance correlations in sequences, as demonstrated in the following diagram:

The GRU is much more complex in shape than the regular recurrent layer. There are a lot more lines connecting different inputs to the output. Let's go over the diagram and take a look at what the general idea is behind this layer type.

Unlike the regular recurrent layer, the GRU layer has an **update gate** and **reset gate**. The reset and update gates are the valves that control how much of the memory of previous time steps is kept, and how much of the new data is used for producing the new memory.

Predicting output is very similar to predicting with a regular recurrent layer. When we feed data into the layer, the previous hidden state is used to calculate the value for the new hidden state. When all elements in the sequence have been processed, the output is calculated using one additional set of weights, just as we did in the regular recurrent layer.

Calculating the hidden state over multiple time steps is a lot more complicated in a GRU. There are a few steps needed to update the hidden state of the GRU. First, we need to calculate the value for the update gate as follows:

$$z_t = sigmoid(W^{(z)} x_t + U^{(z)} h_{t-1})$$

The update gate is controlled using two sets of weights, one for the hidden state from the previous time step, and one for the current input provided to the layer. The value produced by the update gate controls how much of the past time steps is kept in the hidden state.

The second step is to update the reset gate. This is done using the following formula:

$$r_t = sigmoid(W^{(r)} x_t + U^{(r)} h_{t-1})$$

The reset gate is also controlled using two sets of weights; one for the input value for the current time step and another set of weights for the hidden state. The reset gate controls how much of the hidden state is removed. This becomes clear when we calculate an initial version of the new hidden state as follows:

$$'h_t = tanh(W x_t + r_t \odot U h_{t-1})$$

First, we multiply the input with its corresponding weights. Then, we multiply the previous hidden state with its corresponding weights. We then calculate the element-wise or Hadamard product between the reset gate and the weighted hidden state. Finally, we add this to the weighted input, and use a `tanh` activation over this to calculate the remembered hidden state.

The reset gate in this formula controls how much is forgotten of the previous hidden state. A reset gate with a low value will remove a lot of data from the previous time step. A higher value will help the layer remember a lot from the previous time step.

We're not done yet though—once we have the information coming from the previous timestamp increased by the update gate and tempered by the reset gate, this produces the remembered information from the previous time step. We can now calculate the final hidden state value based on this remembered information as follows:

$$h_t = z_t \odot h_{t-1} + (1 - z_t) \odot 'h_t$$

First, we take the element-wise product between the previous hidden state and the update gate to determine how much information from the previous state should be kept. Then we add to that the element-wise product between the update gate and the remembered information from the previous state. Note that the update gate is used to feed a percentage of new information and a percentage of old information. That's why we're using a *1-* operation in the second part of the formula.

The GRU is a large step up from the recurrent layer in terms of the calculations involved and its capability to remember long-term and short-term relationships. However, it cannot do both at the same time.

Working with long short-term memory units

Another alternative to working with basic recurrent layers is to use a **Long Short-Term Memory (LSTM)** unit. This recurrent layer works with gates just like the GRU that we discussed in the previous section, except the LSTM has a lot more gates.

The following diagram outlines the structure of the LSTM layer:

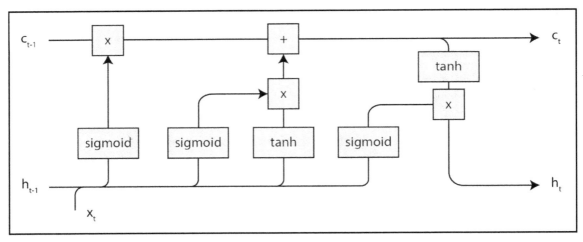

The LSTM unit has a cell state that is central to how this layer type works. The cell state is kept over long periods of time and doesn't change much. The LSTM layer also has a hidden state, but this state serves a different role in the layer.

In short, the LSTM has a long-term memory modeled as the cell state, and a short-term memory modeled as the hidden state. The access to the long-term memory is guarded using several gates. There are two gates that control the long-term memory access in the LSTM layer:

- The forget gate, which controls what will be forgotten from the cell state
- The input gate, which controls what will be stored from the hidden state and input in the cell state

There's one final gate in the LSTM layer that controls what to take from the cell state into the new hidden state. Essentially, we're using the output gate to control what to take from long-term memory into short-term memory. Let's go over how the layer works step by step.

First, we'll take a look at the forget gate. The forget gate is the first gate that will get updated when you make a prediction with an LSTM layer:

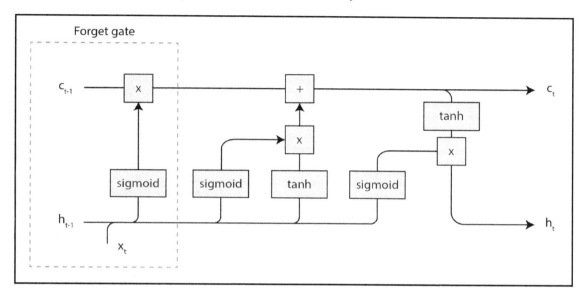

The forget gate controls how much of the cell state should be forgotten. It is updated with the following formula:

$$f_t = sigmoid(W_f[h_{t-1}, x+t] + b_f)$$

When you take a closer look at this formula, you will notice that it is essentially a dense layer with a `sigmoid` activation function. The forget gate generates a vector with values between zero and one to control how much of the elements in the cell state are forgotten. A value of one on the forget gate means that the value in the cell state is kept. A value of zero on the forget gate makes the cell state forget its value.

We're concatenating the hidden state from the previous step and the new input into one matrix along the column axis. The cell state will essentially store long-term information about the input provided to the layer with the hidden state that was stored in the layer.

The second gate in the LSTM layer is the input gate. The input gate controls how much new data is stored in the cell state. The new data is a combination of the hidden state from the previous step and the input for the current time step, as is demonstrated in the following diagram:

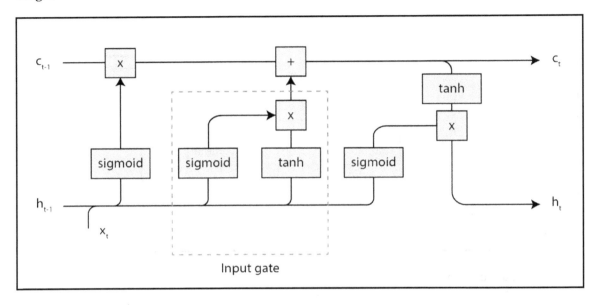

Input gate

We'll use the following formula to determine the value for the update gate:

$$i_t = sigmoid(W_i[h_{t-1}, x_t] + b_i)$$

Just like the forget gate, the input gate is modeled as a nested dense layer within the LSTM layer. You can see the input gate as the left branch within the highlighted section of the previous diagram. The input gate is used in the following formula to determine the new value to put into the cell state:

$$\tilde{c}_t = tanh(W_c[h_{t-1}, x_t] + b_c)$$

To update the cell state, we need one more step, which is highlighted in the next diagram:

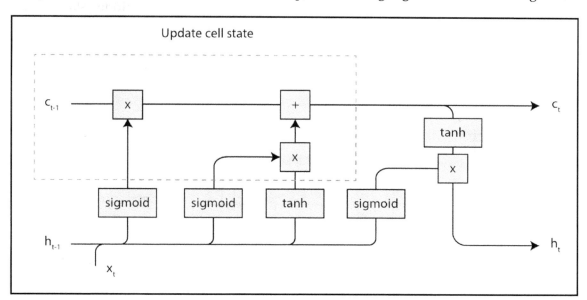

Once we know the values for the forget gate and input gate, we can calculate the updated cell state using the following formula:

$$c_t = f_t * c_{t-1} + i_t * \tilde{c}_t$$

First, we'll multiply the forget gate with the previous cell state to forget old information. We then multiply the update gate with the new values for the cell state to learn new information. We sum both values up to produce the final cell state for the current time step.

The final gate in the LSTM layer is the output gate. This gate controls how much information from the cell state is used in the output of the layer and the hidden state for the next time step, as demonstrated in the following diagram:

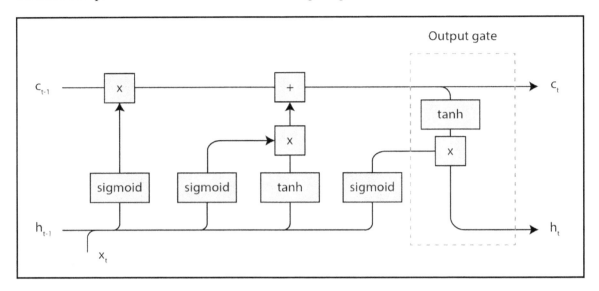

The output gate is calculated using the following formula:

$$o_t = sigmoid(W_o[h_{t-1}, x_t] + b_o)$$

The output gate is, just like the input gate and forget gate, a dense layer that controls how much of the cell state is copied to the output. We can now calculate the new hidden state, or output, of the layer using the following formula:

$$h_t = o_t * tanh(c_t)$$

You can use this new hidden state to calculate the next time step, or return it as the output for the layer.

When to use other recurrent layer types

The GRU and LSTM layers are definitely more complex than regular recurrent layers. They have a lot more parameters that need to be trained. This will make it harder to debug the model when you run into problems.

The regular recurrent layer doesn't hold up well when you work with longer sequences of data, because it gets saturated quickly. You can use both the LSTM and GRU to resolve this problem. The GRU layer works without an additional memory state. The LSTM uses a cell state to model long-term memory.

Because the GRU has fewer gates and no memory, it takes less time to train it. So, if you're looking to process longer sequences and need a network that can be trained relatively quickly, use the GRU layer.

The LSTM layer has more power to express relationships in the sequences you feed it. This means that it will perform better if you have enough data to train it. In the end, it comes down to experimentation to determine which layer type works best for your solution.

Building recurrent neural networks with CNTK

Now that we've explored the theory behind recurrent neural networks, it's time to build one with CNTK. There are several building blocks that CNTK offers for building recurrent neural networks. We're going to explore how to build a recurrent neural network using a sample dataset containing power measurements from a solar panel.

The power output of a solar panel changes during the day, so it's hard to predict how much power is generated for a typical house. This makes it hard for a local energy company to predict how much additional power they should generate to keep up with demand.

Luckily, many energy companies offer software that allows customers to keep track of the power output of their solar panels. This will allow them to train a model based on this historical data, so we can predict what the total power output will be per day.

We're going to train a power output prediction model using recurrent neural networks based on a dataset offered by Microsoft as part of the CNTK documentation.

The dataset contains multiple measurements per day, and contains the current power output at a timestamp, and the total amount of power produced up to that timestamp. It's our goal to predict the total power produced for a day, based on the measurements collected during the day.

You can use a regular neural network, but that would mean that we would have to turn each collected measurement into a feature for the input. Doing so assumes that there's no correlation between the measurements. But, in practice, there is. Each future measurement depends on a measurement that came before. So, a recurrent model that can reason over time is much more practical for this case.

In the next three sections we'll explore how to build a recurrent neural network in CNTK. After that we'll explore how to train the recurrent neural network using data from the solar panel dataset. Finally, we'll take a look how to predict output with a recurrent neural network.

Building the neural network structure

Before we can start to make predictions about the output of a solar panel we need to construct a recurrent neural network. A recurrent neural network is built in the same fashion as a regular neural network. Here's how to build one:

```
features = sequence.input_variable(1)

with default_options(initial_state = 0.1):
    model = Sequential([
        Fold(LSTM(15)),
        Dense(1)
    ])(features)
target = input_variable(1, dynamic_axes=model.dynamic_axes)
```

Follow the given steps:

1. First, create a new input variable to store the input sequence.
2. Then, initialize the default_options for the neural network and provide the initial_state setting with a value of 0.1.
3. Next, Create a Sequential layer set for the neural network.
4. In the Sequential layer set, provide a LSTM recurrent layer with 15 neurons wrapped in a Fold layer.
5. Finally, add a Dense layer with one neuron.

There are two ways in which you can model recurrent neural networks in CNTK. If you're only interested in the final output of a recurrent layer, you can use the `Fold` layer combined with a recurrent layer, such as GRU, LSTM, or even RNNStep. The `Fold` layer collects the final hidden state of the recurrent layer, and returns that as the output to be used by the next layer.

As an alternative to the `Fold` layer, you can also use the `Recurrence` block. This wrapper returns the full sequence generated by the recurrent layer you wrap in it. This is useful if you want to generate sequential output with your recurrent neural network.

A recurrent neural network works with sequential input, this is why we're using the `sequence.input_variable` function instead of a regular `input_variable` function.

The regular `input_variable` function supports only fixed dimensions for the input. This means that we have to know the number of features that we want to feed into the network for each sample. This applies to both regular models and models that process images. In image classification models, we typically use one dimension for color channels, and another two dimensions for the width and height of the input image. We know all these dimensions upfront. The only dimension that is dynamic in the regular `input_variable` function is the batch dimension. This dimension gets calculated when you train the model with a certain minibatch size setting, which results in a fixed value for the batch dimension.

In recurrent neural networks, we don't know how long each sequence will be. We only know the shape of each piece of data stored in the sequence as a time step. The `sequence.input_variable` function allows us to provide the dimensions for each time step, and keep the dimension that models the sequence length dynamic. As with the regular `input_variable` function, the batch dimension is also dynamic. We configure this dimension when we start training with a particular minibatch size setting.

CNTK is unique in the way it handles sequential data. In frameworks such as TensorFlow, you have to specify the dimensions for both the sequence length and batch upfront, before you can start training. Because you have to use fixed size sequences, you will need to add padding to sequences that are shorter than the maximum sequence length supported by your model. Also, if you have longer sequences, you need to truncate them. This leads to lower quality models, because you ask the model to learn information from empty time steps in your sequence. CNTK handles dynamic sequences quite well, so you don't have to use padding when working with sequences in CNTK.

Stacking multiple recurrent layers

In the previous section, we only talked about using a single recurrent layer. You can, however, stack multiple recurrent layers in CNTK. For example, when we want to stack two recurrent layers, we need to use the following combination of layers:

```
from cntk import sequence, default_options, input_variable
from cntk.layers import Recurrence, LSTM, Dropout, Dense, Sequential, Fold,
Recurrence

features = sequence.input_variable(1)

with default_options(initial_state = 0.1):
    model = Sequential([
        Recurrence(LSTM(15)),
        Fold(LSTM(15)),
        Dense(1)
    ])(features)
```

Follow the given steps:

1. First, import the `sequence` module, `default_options` function and `input_variable` function from the `cntk` package
2. Next, import the layers for the recurrent neural network
3. Then, create a new `LSTM` layer with 15 neurons and wrap it in a `Recurrence` layer so the layer returns a sequence instead of a single output
4. Now, create the second `LSTM` layer with 15 neurons, but this time wrap it in a `Fold` layer to return only the final time step as output
5. Finally, invoke the created `Sequential` layer stack with the features variable to complete the neural network

This technique can be extended beyond two layers as well; just wrap the layers before the last recurrent layer in `Recurrence` layers and wrap the final layer in a `Fold` layer.

For the sample in this chapter we'll limit ourselves to using one recurrent layer as we've constructed it in the previous section, *Building the neural network structure*. In the next section we'll talk about training the recurrent neural network that we've created.

Training the neural network with time series data

Now that we have a model, let's take a look at how to train a recurrent neural network in CNTK.

First, we need to define what loss function we want to optimize. Since we're predicting a continuous variable—power output—we need to use a mean squared error loss. We'll combine the loss with a mean square error metric to measure the performance of our model. Remember, from Chapter 4, *Validating Model Performance,* that we can combine the loss and metric in a single function object using @Function:

```
@Function
def criterion_factory(z, t):
    loss = squared_error(z, t)
    metric = squared_error(z, t)
    return loss, metric

loss = criterion_factory(model, target)
learner = adam(model.parameters, lr=0.005, momentum=0.9)
```

We're going to use the adam learner to optimize the model. This learner is an extension of the **Stochastic Gradient Descent** (**SGD**) algorithm. While SGD uses a fixed learning rate, Adam changes the learning rate over time. In the beginning, it will use a high learning rate to get results fast. Once it has run for a while, it will start to lower the learning rate to increase accuracy. The adam optimizer is a lot faster than SGD in optimizing the loss function.

Now we have a loss, metric, we can use both in-memory and out-of-memory data to train the recurrent neural network.

The data for a recurrent neural network needs to be modeled as sequences. In our case, the input data is a sequence of power measurements for each day, stored in a **CNTK Text Format** (**CTF**) file.Follow the given steps:

In Chapter 3, *Getting Data into Your Neural Network,* we discussed how you can store data for training in CNTK in CTF format. The CTF file format not only supports storing basic samples, but also supports storing sequences. A CTF file for sequences has the following layout:

```
<sequence_id> |<input_name> <values> |<input_name> <values>
```

Each line is prefixed with a unique number to identify the sequence. CNTK will consider lines with the same sequence identifier to be one sequence. So, you can store one sequence over multiple lines. Each line can contain one time step in the sequence.

There's one important detail you have to keep in mind when storing sequences over multiple lines in a CTF file. One of the lines storing the sequence should also contain the expected output for the sequence. Let's take a look at what that looks like in practice:

```
0  |target 0.837696335078534  |features 0.756544502617801
0  |features 0.7931937172774869
0  |features 0.8167539267015707
0  |features 0.8324607329842932
0  |features 0.837696335078534
0  |features 0.837696335078534
0  |features 0.837696335078534
1  |target 0.4239092495636999  |features 0.24554973821989529
1  |features 0.24554973821989529
1  |features 0.00017225130534296885
1  |features 0.0014886562154347149
1  |features 0.005673647442829338
1  |features 0.01481675392670157
```

The first line for a sequence contains the `target` variable, as well as the data for the first time step in the sequence. The `target` variable is used to store the expected power output for a particular sequence. The other lines for the same sequence only contain the `features` variable. You can't use the input file if you do put the `target` variable on a separate line. The minibatch source will fail to load.

You can load the sequence data into your training code, like so:

```
def create_datasource(filename, sweeps=INFINITELY_REPEAT):
    target_stream = StreamDef(field='target', shape=1, is_sparse=False)
    features_stream = StreamDef(field='features', shape=1, is_sparse=False)

    deserializer = CTFDeserializer(filename,
StreamDefs(features=features_stream, target=target_stream))
    datasource = MinibatchSource(deserializer, randomize=True,
max_sweeps=sweeps)
    return datasource

train_datasource = create_datasource('solar_train.ctf')
test_datasource = create_datasource('solar_val.ctf', sweeps=1)
```

Follow the given steps:

1. First, create a new function create_datasource with two parameters: filename, and sweeps which has a default of INFINITELY_REPEAT so we can iterate over the same dataset multiple times.
2. In the `create_datasource` function, define two streams for the minibatch source, one for the input features and one for the expected output of our model.
3. Then use `CTFDeserializer` to read the input file.
4. Finally, return a new `MinibatchSource` for the input file provided.

To train the model, we need to iterate over the same data multiple times to train for multiple epochs. That's why you should use an infinity setting for the `max_sweeps` of the minibatch source. Testing is done by iterating over a set of validation samples so that we configure the minibatch source with just one sweep.

Let's train the neural network with the data sources provided, as follows:

```
progress_writer = ProgressPrinter(0)
test_config = TestConfig(test_datasource)

input_map = {
    features: train_datasource.streams.features,
    target: train_datasource.streams.target
}

history = loss.train(
    train_datasource,
    epoch_size=EPOCH_SIZE,
    parameter_learners=[learner],
    model_inputs_to_streams=input_map,
    callbacks=[progress_writer, test_config],
    minibatch_size=BATCH_SIZE,
    max_epochs=EPOCHS)
```

Follow the given steps:

1. First, initialize a `ProgressPrinter` to log the output of the training process.
2. Then, create a new test configuration to validate the neural network using data from the `test_datasource`.
3. Next, Create a mapping between the input variables of the neural network and the streams from the training datasource.
4. Finally, invoke the train method on the loss function to start the training process. Provide it the `train_datasource`, settings, the learner, `input_map` and the callbacks for logging and testing.

The model needs to train for quite a long time, so grab yourself a coffee or two when you plan to run the sample code on your machine.

The `train` method will output the metrics and loss values on screen, because we used `ProgressPrinter` as a callback for the `train` method. The output will look similar to this:

average loss	since last	average metric	since last	examples
Learning rate per minibatch: 0.005				
0.66	0.66	0.66	0.66	19
0.637	0.626	0.637	0.626	59
0.699	0.752	0.699	0.752	129
0.676	0.656	0.676	0.656	275
0.622	0.573	0.622	0.573	580
0.577	0.531	0.577	0.531	1150

As good practice, you want to validate your model against a separate test set. That's why we created the `test_datasource` function earlier. To use this data to validate your model, you can use a `TestConfig` object as a callback for the `train` method. The testing logic will be called automatically when the training process is completed.

Predicting output

When the model is finally done training, you can test it using a few sample sequences that can be found in the sample code for this chapter. Remember, a CNTK model is a function, so you can invoke it with a numpy array representing the sequence for which you want to predict the total output, as follows:

```
import pickle

NORMALIZE = 19100

with open('test_samples.pkl', 'rb') as test_file:
    test_samples = pickle.load(test_file)
model(test_samples) * NORMALIZE
```

Follow the given steps:

1. First, import the pickle package
2. Next, define the settings to normalize the data
3. After that, open the test_samples.pkl file for reading.

4. Once the file is opened, load its contents using the pickle.load function.
5. Finally, run the samples through the network and multiply them with the NORMALIZE constant to obtain the predicted output for the solar panel.

The output produced by the model is between zero and one, because that's what we stored in the original dataset. The values represent a normalized version of the power output of the solar panel. We need to multiply them by the normalization value that we used to normalize the original measurements to get the actual power output of the solar panel.

The final denormalized output for the model looks like this:

```
array([[ 8161.595],
       [16710.596],
       [13220.489],
       ...,
       [10979.5  ],
       [15410.741],
       [16656.523]], dtype=float32)
```

Predicting with a recurrent neural network is pretty similar to making predictions with any other CNTK model, except for the fact that you need to provide sequences rather than single samples.

Summary

In this chapter, we've looked at how to use recurrent neural networks to make predictions based on time series data. Recurrent neural networks are useful in scenarios where you have to deal with financial data, IoT data, or any other information that is collected over time.

One important building block for recurrent neural networks is the Fold and the Recurrence layer types, which you can combine with any of the recurrent layer types, such as RNNStep, GRU, or LSTM, to build a recurrent layer set. Depending on whether you want to predict a sequence or single value, you can use the Recurrence or Fold layer types to wrap the recurrent layers.

When you're training a recurrent neural network, you can make use of the sequence data stored in the CTF file format to make it easier to train the model. But, you can just as easily use sequences stored as numpy arrays, as long as you use the correct combination of sequence input variables with recurrent layers.

Making predictions with a recurrent neural network is just as easy as it is for regular neural networks. The only difference is the input data format, which is, just as for training, a sequence.

In the next chapter, we'll look at one last topic for this book: *Deploying Models to Production*. We'll explore how to use CNTK models you've built in C# or Java, and how to properly manage your experiments using tools such as the Azure Machine Learning service.

Deploying Models to Production 7

In the previous chapters of this book, we've worked on our skills for developing, testing, and using various deep learning models. We haven't talked much about the role of deep learning within the broader context of software engineering. In this last chapter, we will use the time to talk about continuous delivery, and the role of machine learning within this context. We will then look at how you can deploy models to production with a continuous delivery mindset. Finally, we will look at Azure Machine Learning service to properly manage the models you develop.

The following topics will be covered in this chapter:

- Using machine learning in a DevOps environment
- Storing models
- Using Azure Machine Learning service to manage models

Technical requirements

We assume that you have a recent version of Anaconda installed on your computer, and have followed the steps in `Chapter 1`, *Getting Started with CNTK,* to install CNTK on your computer. The sample code for this chapter can be found in our GitHub repository at: `https://github.com/PacktPublishing/Deep-Learning-with-Microsoft-Cognitive-Toolkit-Quick-Start-Guide/tree/master/ch7`.

In this chapter, we'll work on a few examples stored in Jupyter notebooks. To access the sample code, run the following commands inside an Anaconda prompt in the directory where you've downloaded the code:

```
cd ch7
jupyter notebook
```

This chapter also contains a C# code sample to demonstrate how to load models in the open source ONNX format. If you want to run the C# code you will need to have .NET Core 2.2 installed on your machine. You can download the latest version of .NET core from: `https://dotnet.microsoft.com/download`.

Check out the following video to see the code in action:

`http://bit.ly/2U8YkZf`

Using machine learning in a DevOps environment

Most modern software development happens in an agile fashion, in an environment where developers and IT-pros work on the same project. The software we're building often is deployed to production through continuous integration and continuous deployment pipelines. How are we going to integrate machine learning in this modern environment? And does it mean we have to change a lot when we start building AI solutions? These are some of the frequently asked questions you can run into when you introduce AI and machine learning to the workflow.

Luckily, you don't have to change your whole build environment or deployment tool stack to integrate machine learning into your software. Most of the things that we'll talk about will fit right into your existing environment.

Let's take a look at a typical continuous delivery scenario that you may encounter in a regular agile software project:

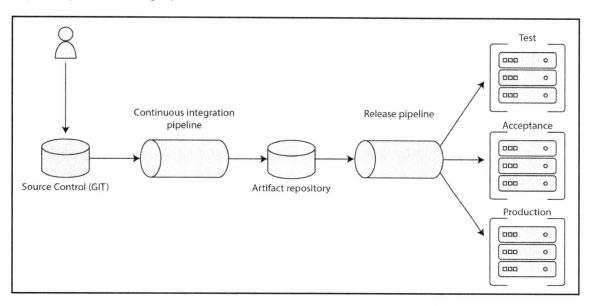

This overview will look familiar if you've worked in a DevOps environment before. It starts with source control, which is connected to a continuous integration pipeline. The continuous integration pipeline produces artifacts that can be deployed to production. These artifacts are typically stored somewhere for backup and rollback purposes. This artifact repository is connected to a release pipeline that deploys the software to a test, acceptance, and, finally, a production environment.

You don't need to change much of this standard setup to integrate machine learning into it. There are, however, a few key things that are important to get right when you start to use machine learning. Let's focus on four stages and explore how to extend the standard continuous delivery setup:

- How to keep track of the data you use for machine learning.
- Training models in a continuous integration pipeline.
- Deploying models to production.
- Gathering feedback on production.

Keeping track of your data

Let's start where it all begins with machine learning: the data with which you are going to train your models. It's difficult to get good data for machine learning. Almost 80% of your effort will be on data management and data processing. It would be really sad if you had to redo all your work every time you want to train a model.

That's why it is important to have some form of data management in place. This can be a central server where you store datasets that you know are good to use for training models. It could also be a data warehouse, if you have more than a few gigabytes of data. Some companies choose to use tools such as Hadoop or Azure Data Lake to manage their data. Whatever you use, the most important thing is to keep your dataset clean and in a format that is ready to use for training.

To create a data pipeline for your solution you can use traditional **Extract Transform Load** (**ETL**) tools, such as SQL server integration services, or you can build custom scripts in Python and execute them as part of a dedicated continuous integration pipeline in Jenkins, Azure DevOps, or Team Foundation Server.

The data pipeline will be your tool to gather data from various business sources, and process it so that you get a dataset that is of sufficient quality to be stored as the master dataset for your model. It's important to note here that, although you can reuse datasets across different models, it is best not to start out with this goal in mind. You will quickly find that your master dataset will turn dirty and unmanageable when you try to use the dataset across too many usage scenarios.

Training models in a continuous integration pipeline

Once you have a basic data pipeline running, it's time to look at integrating the training of AI models in your continuous integration environment. Up until now, we've only used Python notebooks to create our models. Sadly, Python notebooks don't deploy well to production. You can't automatically run them during a build.

In a continuous delivery environment, you can still use Python notebooks to perform initial experiments in order to discover patterns in the data and to build an initial version of your model. Once you have a candidate model, you will have to move your code away from a notebook and into a proper Python program.

You can run your Python training code as part of a continuous integration pipeline. For example, if you're using Azure DevOps, Team Foundation Server, or Jenkins, you already have all the tools to run your training code as a continuous integration pipeline.

We recommend running the training code as a separate pipeline from the rest of your software. Training a deep learning model often takes a very long time, and you don't want to lock your build infrastructure on that. Often, you will see people build training pipelines for their machine learning models using dedicated virtual machines, or even dedicated hardware, because of the amount of computation power it takes to train a model.

The continuous integration pipeline will produce a model based on a dataset you produced using your data pipeline. Just like code, you should also version your models and the settings you've used to train them.

Keeping track of your models and the settings you used to train them is important, as this allows you to experiment with different versions of the same model in production and gather feedback. Keeping a backup of your trained models also helps to get back in production fast after a disaster, such as a crashed production server.

Since models are binary files and can get quite large, it's best you treat your models as binary artifacts, much like NuGet packages in .NET, or Maven artifacts in Java.

Tools like Nexus or Artifactory are great for storing models. Publishing your models in Nexus or Artifactory takes only a few lines of code, and will save you up to hundreds of hours of work retraining your model.

Deploying models to production

Once you have a model, you need to be able to deploy it to production. If you've stored your models in a repository, such as Artifactory or Nexus, this becomes easier. You can create dedicated release pipelines in the same way that you would create a continuous integration pipeline. In Azure DevOps and Team Foundation Server, there's a dedicated feature for this. In Jenkins, you can use a separate pipeline to deploy models to a server.

In the release pipeline, you can download your model from the artifact repository and deploy it to production. There are two main deployment methods for machine learning models. Either you can deploy it as an extra file with your application, or you can deploy it as a dedicated service component.

If you're deploying your model as part of an application, you will typically store just the model in your artifact repository. The model now becomes an extra artifact that needs to be downloaded in an existing release pipeline that deploys your solution.

If you're deploying a dedicated service component for your model, you will typically store the model, the scripts that use the model to make a prediction, and other files needed by the model, in the artifact repository and deploy that to production.

Gathering feedback on your models

There's one last point that is important to keep in mind when working with deep learning or machine learning models in production. You've trained the models with a certain dataset. You hope this dataset contains a good representation of what is really happening in your production environment. But it doesn't have to be that way, because the world changes around you as you build your models.

That's why it is important to ask for feedback from your users and update your model accordingly. Although not officially part of a continuous deployment environment, it's still an important aspect to set up correctly if you want to be successful with your machine learning solution.

Setting up a feedback loop doesn't have to be very complicated. For example, when you're classifying transactions for fraud detection, you can set up a feedback loop by asking an employee to validate the outcome of the model. You can then store the validation result of the employee with the input that was classified. By doing this, you make sure your model doesn't falsely accuse customers of fraud, and it helps you gather new observations to improve your model. Later, when you want to improve the model, you can use the newly gathered observations to extend your training set.

Storing your models

In order to be able to deploy your models to production, you need to be able to store a trained model on disk. CNTK offers two ways to store models on disk. You can either store checkpoints to continue training at a later time, or you can store a portable version of your model. Each of these storage methods has its own use.

Storing model checkpoints to continue training at a later point

Some models take a long time to train, sometimes up to weeks at a time. You don't want to lose all your progress when your machine crashes during training, or if there's a power outage.

This is where checkpointing becomes useful. You can create a checkpoint during training using a `CheckpointConfig` object. You can add this additional callback to your training code by modifying the callbacks list as follows:

```
checkpoint_config = CheckpointConfig('solar.dnn', frequency=100,
restore=True, preserve_all=False)

history = loss.train(
    train_datasource,
    epoch_size=EPOCH_SIZE,
    parameter_learners=[learner],
    model_inputs_to_streams=input_map,
    callbacks=[progress_writer, test_config, checkpoint_config],
    minibatch_size=BATCH_SIZE,
    max_epochs=EPOCHS)
```

Follow the given steps:

1. First, create a new `CheckpointConfig` and provide a filename for the checkpointed model file, the number of minibatches before a new checkpoint should be created as the `frequency` and set the `preserve_all` setting to `False`.
2. Next, use the train method on the `loss` and provide the `checkpoint_config` in the `callbacks` keyword argument to use checkpointing.

When you use checkpointing during training, you will start to see additional files on disk named `solar.dnn`, and `solar.dnn.ckp`. The `solar.dnn` file contains the trained model stored in a binary format. The `solar.dnn.ckp` file contains the checkpoint information for the minibatch source used during training.

The most recent checkpoint is automatically restored for you when you set the restore parameter of the `CheckpointConfig` object to `True`. This makes it easy to integrate checkpointing in your training code.

Having a checkpointed model is not only useful in case you run into a computer problem during training. A checkpoint is also useful if you want to continue training after you've gathered additional data from production. You can simply restore the latest checkpoint and start feeding new samples into the model from there.

Storing portable models for use in other applications

Although you can use a checkpointed model in production, it's not very smart to do so. Checkpointed models are stored in a format that is only understood by CNTK. For now, it's fine to use the binary format, since CNTK is around and the model format will remain compatible for quite a long time. But, as with all software, CNTK isn't made to last for an eternity.

That's exactly why ONNX was invented. ONNX is the open neural network exchange format. When you use ONNX, you store your model in a protobuf compatible format that is understood by many other frameworks. There's even a native ONNX runtime available for Java and C#, which allows you to use models created in CNTK from your .NET or Java application.

ONNX is supported by a number of large companies, such as Facebook, Intel, NVIDIA, Microsoft, AMD, IBM, and Hewlett-Packard. Some of these companies offer converters for ONNX, while others even support running ONNX models directly on their hardware without using additional software. NVIDIA has a number of chips available now that can read ONNX files directly and execute these models.

As an example, we'll first explore how to store a model in the ONNX format and use C# to load it from disk again to make predictions. First, we'll look at how to save a model in the ONNX format and after that we'll explore how to load ONNX models.

Storing a model in ONNX format

To store a model in the ONNX format you can use the `save` method on the `model` function. When you don't provide any additional parameters, it will store the model in the same format as is used for checkpointing. You can, however, provide an additional parameter to specify the model format as follows:

```
from cntk import ModelFormat

model.save('solar.onnx', format=ModelFormat.ONNX)
```

Follow the given steps:

1. First, import the `ModelFormat` enumeration from the `cntk` package.
2. Next, invoke the `save` method on the trained model with the output filename and specify `ModelFormat.ONNX` as the `format` keyword argument.

Using ONNX models in C#

Once the model is stored on disk, we can use C# to load and use it. CNTK version 2.6 includes a pretty complete API for C#, which you can use for training and evaluating models.

To use a CNTK model in C# you need to use a library called `CNTK.GPU` or `CNTK.CPUOnly`, which can be retrieved from NuGet, a package manager for .NET. The CPU-only version of CNTK includes a version of the CNTK binaries that have been compiled to run models on the CPU, while the GPU version can use the GPU as well as the CPU.

Loading a CNTK model in C# is done by using the following snippet of code:

```
var deviceDescriptor = DeviceDescriptor.CPUDevice;
var function = Function.Load("model.onnx", deviceDescriptor,
ModelFormat.ONNX);
```

Follow the given steps:

1. First, create a device descriptor so the model is executed against the CPU.
2. Next, use the `Function.Load` method to load the previously stored model. Provide the `deviceDescriptor` and use the `ModelFormat.ONNX` to load the file as ONNX model.

Now that we have loaded the model, let's make a prediction with it. For, this we need to write another fragment of code:

```
public IList<float> Predict(float petalWidth, float petalLength, float
sepalWidth, float sepalLength)
{
    var features = _modelFunction.Inputs[0];
    var output = _modelFunction.Outputs[0];

    var inputMapping = new Dictionary<Variable, Value>();
    var outputMapping = new Dictionary<Variable, Value>();

    var batch = Value.CreateBatch(
        features.Shape,
```

```
        new float[] { sepalLength, sepalWidth, petalLength, petalWidth },
        _deviceDescriptor);

    inputMapping.Add(features, batch);
    outputMapping.Add(output, null);

    _modelFunction.Evaluate(inputMapping, outputMapping,
_deviceDescriptor);

    var outputValues = outputMapping[output].GetDenseData<float>(output);
    return outputValues[0];
}
```

Follow the given steps:

1. Create a new method `Predict` that accepts the input features for the model.
2. Within the `Predict` method, store the input and output variable of the model in two separate variables for easy access.
3. Next, create a dictionary to map data to the input and output variables of the model.
4. Then, create a new batch, containing one sample with the input features for the model.
5. Add a new entry to the input mapping to map the batch to the input variable.
6. Next, add a new entry to the output mapping for the output variable.
7. Now, invoke the `Evaluate` method on the loaded model with the input, output mapping, and a device descriptor.
8. Finally, extract the output variable from the output mapping and retrieve the data.

The sample code for this chapter includes a basic C# project in .NET core that demonstrates the use of CNTK from a .NET Core project. You can find the sample code in the `csharp-client` folder in the code examples directory for this chapter.

Working with models stored in the ONNX format makes it possible to use Python for training models and C# or another language to run models on production. This is especially useful since the runtime performance of a language like C# is much better than that of Python.

In the next section we'll look at using Azure Machine Learning service to manage the process of training and storing models so we have a much more structured way of working with models.

Using Azure Machine Learning service to manage models

While you can completely hand-build a continuous integration pipeline, it's still quite a bit of work. You need to get dedicated hardware to run deep learning training jobs, and that can bring up the costs. There are great alternatives available in the cloud. Google has a TensorFlow serving offer. Microsoft offers Azure Machine Learning service as a way to manage models. Both are great tools that we can highly recommend.

Let's take a look at Azure Machine Learning service to get a sense of what it can do for you when you want to set up a complete machine learning pipeline:

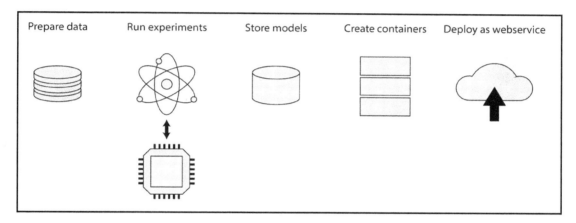

Azure Machine Learning service is a cloud service that offers a complete solution for every phase of your machine learning project. It has the concept of experiments, and runs that allow you to manage experiments. It features a model registry that allows you to store trained models and Docker images for those models. You can use the Azure Machine Learning service tools to deploy these models to production in a matter of minutes.

Deploying Azure Machine Learning service

In order to use this service, you need to have an active account on Azure. You can use a trial account by going to: `https://azure.microsoft.com/en-gb/free/`, if you haven't got an account yet. This will give you a free account for 12 months with 150 dollars, worth of credits to explore the different Azure services.

There are many ways in which you can deploy Azure Machine Learning service. You can create a new instance through the portal, but you can also use the cloud shell to create an instance of the service. Let's take a look at how you can create a new Azure Machine Learning service instance through the portal.

With your favorite browser, navigate to the URL at: `https://portal.azure.com/`. Log in with your credentials, and you will be greeted with a portal that shows you all your available Azure resources and a dashboard resembling the following screenshot:

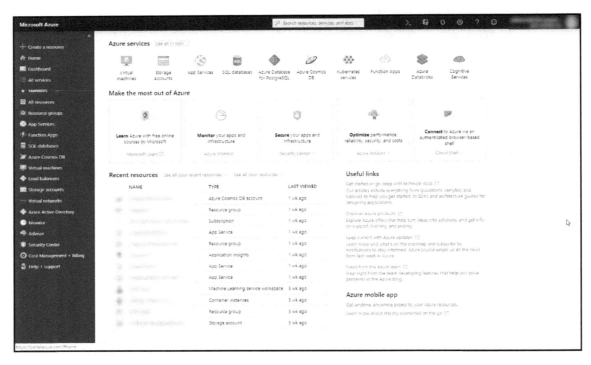

Azure resources and a dashboard

From this portal you can create new Azure resources, such as the Azure Machine Learning Workspace. Click the large + button at the top left of the screen to get started. This will show the following page, allowing you to create a new resource:

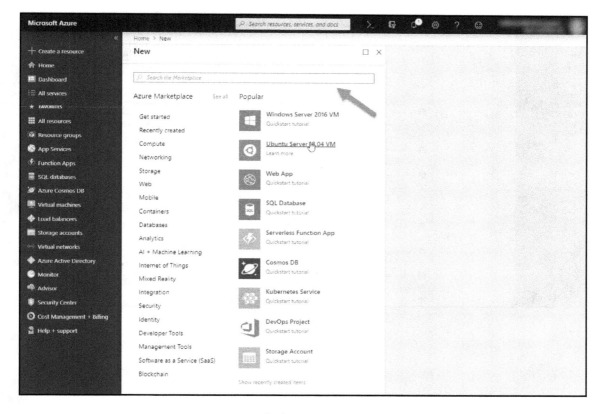

Creating a new resource

You can search for different types of resources in this search bar. Search for **Azure Machine Learning** and select the **Azure Machine Learning Workspace** resource type from the list. This will show the following details panel that allows you to start the creation wizard:

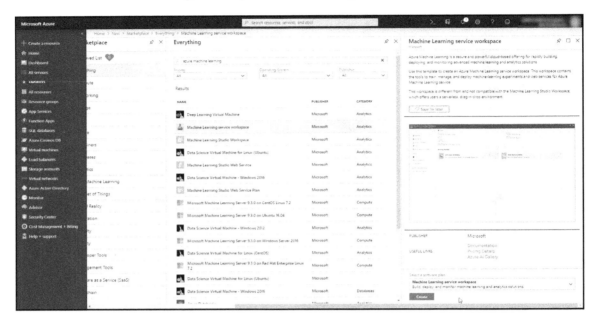

Starting the creation wizard

This details panel will explain what the resource does, and point towards the documentation and other important information about this resource, such as the pricing details. To create a new instance of this resource type, click the **create** button. This will start the wizard to create a new instance of the Azure Machine Learning workspace as follows:

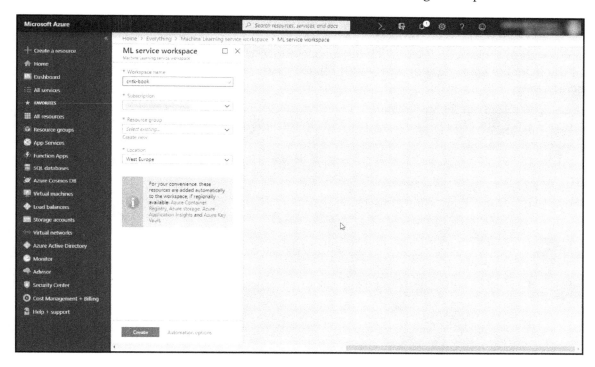

Creating a new instance of the Azure Machine Learning workspace

In the creation wizard, you can configure the name of the workspace, the resource group it belongs to, and the data center it should create. Azure resources are created as part of resource groups. These resource groups help you organize things, and keep related infrastructure together in one place. If you want to remove a set of resources, you can just delete the resource group instead of every resource separately. This is especially useful if you want to remove everything after you're done testing the machine learning workspace.

It's a good idea to use a dedicated resource group for the machine learning workspace, since it will contain more than one resource. Mixing this with other resources will make it harder to clean up after you're done or need to move resources for some reason.

Once you have clicked the **create** button at the bottom of the screen, the machine learning workspace is created. This will take a few minutes. In the background, the Azure Resource Manager will create a number of resources based on the selection in the creation wizard. You will receive a notification in the portal when the deployment is completed.

When the machine learning workspace is created, you can navigate to the workspace through the portal by first going to the **Resource groups** on the portal in the navigation bar on the left of the screen. Next, click the resource group you just created to get an overview of the machine learning workspace and related resources, as shown in the following screenshot:

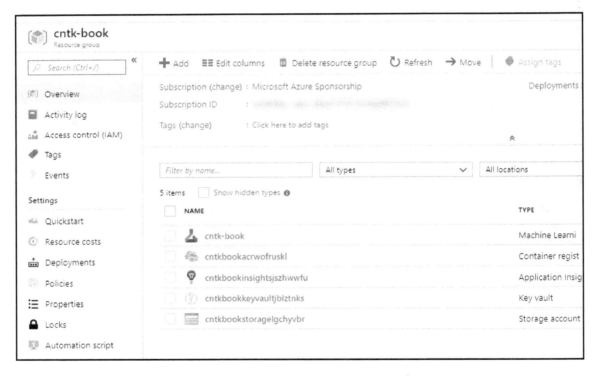

Getting an overview of the machine learning workspace and related resources

There's the workspace itself, with a dashboard that allows you to explore experiments and manage some aspects of your machine learning solution. The workspace also includes a Docker registry to store models as Docker images, together with the scripts needed to make a prediction using a model. When you check out the workspace on Azure Portal, you'll also find a storage account that you can use to store datasets and data generated by your experiments.

One of the nice things that's included in an Azure Machine Learning service environment is an Application Insights instance. You can use Application Insights to monitor your models in production and gather valuable feedback to improve your models later on. This is included by default, so you don't have to manually create a monitoring solution for your machine learning solution.

Exploring the machine learning workspace

The Azure Machine Learning workspace contains a number of elements. Let's explore them to get a feel of what's available to you when you start working with it:

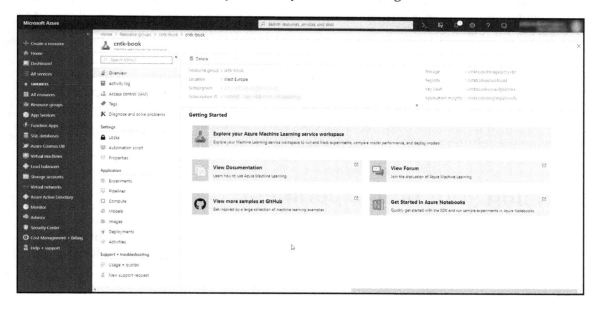

Machine learning workspace

To get to the machine learning workspace, click the **resource groups** item in the navigation bar on the left of the screen. Select the **resource group** containing the **machine learning workspace** item and click on **machine learning workspace**. It will have the name you've configured in the creation wizard earlier.

In the workspace, there's a dedicated section for experiments. This section will provide access to experiments that you've run in the workspace, as well as details about the runs executed as part of the experiments.

Another useful element of the machine learning workspace is the models section. When you've trained a model, you can store it in the model registry so you can deploy it to production at a later time. A model automatically connects to the experiment run that produced it, so you can always trace back what code was used to produce a model, and which settings were used to train it.

Below the model section is the images section. This section shows you the Docker images created from your models. You can package models in Docker images together with a scoring script to make deployment to production easier and more predictable.

Finally, there's the deployment sections that contain all the deployments based on the images. You can use Azure Machine Learning service to deploy models to production using single container instances, a virtual machine, or even a Kubernetes cluster, should you need to scale your model deployment.

Azure Machine Learning service also offers a technique that allows you to build a pipeline to prepare data, train a model, and deploy it to production. This feature can be useful should you want to build a single process that contains both preprocessing steps and training steps. It's especially powerful in cases where you need to execute many steps to obtain a trained model. For now, we'll limit ourselves to running basic experiments and deploying the resulting model to a production Docker container instance.

Running your first experiment

Now that you have a workspace, let's take a look at how to use it from a Python notebook. We'll modify some deep learning code so we save the trained model to the Azure Machine Learning service workspace as the output of an experiment, and track metrics for the model.

First, we need to install the `azureml` package as follows:

```
pip install --upgrade azureml-sdk[notebooks]
```

The `azureml` package contains the necessary components to run experiments. In order for it to work, you'll need to create a file called `config.json` in the root of your machine learning project. If you're working with the sample code for this chapter, you can modify the `config.json` file in the `azure-ml-service` folder. It contains the following content:

```
{
    "workspace_name": "<workspace name>",
    "resource_group": "<resource group>",
    "subscription_id": "<your subscription id>"
}
```

This file contains the workspace your Python code will work with, the resource group that contains the workspace you're working with, and the subscription that the workspace was created in. The workspace name should match the name you've chosen in the wizard to create the workspace earlier. The resource group should match the one that contains the workspace. Finally, you will need to find the subscription ID.

When you navigate to **Resource groups** for the machine learning workspace on the portal, you'll see the **Subscription ID** at the top of the resource group details panel, as shown in the following screenshot:

Subscription ID at the top of the resource group details panel

When you hover over the value for the **Subscription ID**, the portal will show a button to copy the value to your clipboard. Paste this value into the **subscriptionId** field of the config file and save it. You can now connect to your workspace from any Python notebook or Python program by using the following small snippet of code:

```
from azureml.core import Workspace, Experiment

ws = Workspace.from_config()
experiment = Experiment(name='classify-flowers', workspace=ws)
```

Follow the given steps:

1. First, we create a new workspace based on the configuration file we just created. This connects to the workspace in Azure. Once you're connected, you can create a new experiment with a name of your choice and connect it to the workspace.
2. Next, create a new experiment and connect it to the workspace.

An experiment in Azure Machine Learning service can be used to keep track of an architecture you're testing with CNTK. For example, you could create an experiment for a convolutional neural network, and a second experiment to try solving the same problem with a recurrent neural network.

Let's explore how to track metrics and other output from experiments. We'll use the iris flower classification model from previous chapters and extend the training logic to track metrics as follows:

```
from cntk import default_options, input_variable
from cntk.layers import Dense, Sequential
from cntk.ops import log_softmax, sigmoid

model = Sequential([
    Dense(4, activation=sigmoid),
    Dense(3, activation=log_softmax)
])

features = input_variable(4)
z = model(features)
```

Follow the given steps:

1. First, import the default_options and input_variable function.
2. Next, import the layer types for the model from the cntk.layers module.
3. After that, import the log_softmax and sigmoid activation function from the cntk.ops module.
4. Create a new Sequential layer set.
5. Add a new Dense layer to the Sequential layer set with 4 neurons and the sigmoid activation function.
6. Add another Dense layer with 3 outputs and a log_softmax activation function.
7. Create a new input_variable with size 4.
8. Invoke the model with the features variable to complete the model.

To train the model, we're going to use a manual minibatch loop. First, we'll have to load and preprocess the iris dataset so that it matches the format that our model expects, as demonstrated in the following code snippet:

```
import pandas as pd
import numpy as np

df_source = pd.read_csv('iris.csv',
    names=['sepal_length', 'sepal_width','petal_length','petal_width',
'species'],
    index_col=False)

X = df_source.iloc[:, :4].values
y = df_source['species'].values
```

Follow the given steps:

1. Import the `pandas` and `numpy` modules to load the CSV file containing the training samples.
2. Use the read_csv function to load the input file containing the training data.
3. Next, extract the first 4 columns as the input features
4. Finally, extract the species column as the labels

The labels are stored as a string, so we'll have to convert those to a set of one-hot vectors in order to match the model as follows:

```
label_mapping = {
    'Iris-setosa': 0,
    'Iris-versicolor': 1,
    'Iris-virginica': 2
}

def one_hot(index, length):
    result = np.zeros(length)
    result[index] = 1.
y = [one_hot(label_mapping[v], 3) for v in y]
```

Follow the given steps:

1. Create a mapping from labels to their numeric representation.
2. Next, define a new utility function `one_hot` to encode a numeric value to a one-hot vector.
3. Finally, use a python list comprehension, to iterate over the values in the labels collection and turn them into one-hot encoded vectors.

We need to execute one more step to prepare the dataset for training. In order to be able to verify that the model did indeed get optimized correctly, we want to create a hold-out set, against which we will run a test:

```
from sklearn.model_selection import train_test_split

X_train, X_test, y_train, y_test = train_test_split(X,y, test_size=0.2,
stratify=y)
```

Using the `train_test_split` method, create a small hold-out set containing 20% of training samples. Use the `stratify` keyword and provide the labels to balance the split.

Once we have the data prepared, we can focus on training the model. First, we'll need to set up a `loss` function, `learner`, and `trainer` as follows:

```
from cntk.losses import cross_entropy_with_softmax
from cntk.metrics import classification_error
from cntk.learners import sgd
from cntk.train.trainer import Trainer

label = input_variable(3)

loss = cross_entropy_with_softmax(z, label)
error_rate = classification_error(z, label)

learner = sgd(z.parameters, 0.001)
trainer = Trainer(z, (loss, error_rate), [learner])
```

1. Import the cross_entropy_with_softmax function from the `cntk.losses` module.
2. Next, import the classificatin_error function from the `cnkt.metrics` module.
3. Then, import the `sgd` learner from the `cntk.learners` module.
4. Create a new `input_variable` with shape 3 to store the labels
5. Next, create a new instance of the cross_entropy_with_softmax loss and provide it the model variable z and the `label` variable.
6. Then, create a new metric using the classification_error function and provide it the network and `label` variable.
7. Now, initialize the `sgd` learner with the parameters of the network and set its learning rate to 0.001.
8. Finally, initialize the `Trainer` with the network, `loss`, `metric`, and `learner`.

Normally, we could just use the `train` method on the `loss` function to optimize the parameters in our model. This time, however, we want to have control over the training process so we can inject logic to track metrics in the Azure Machine Learning workspace, as demonstrated in the following code snippet:

```
import os
from cntk import ModelFormat

with experiment.start_logging() as run:
    for _ in range(10):
        trainer.train_minibatch({ features: X_train, label: y_train })

        run.log('average_loss', trainer.previous_minibatch_loss_average)
        run.log('average_metric',
trainer.previous_minibatch_evaluation_average)

    test_metric = trainer.test_minibatch( {features: X_test, label: y_test
})
```

Follow the given steps:

1. To start a new run, invoke the `start_logging` method on the experiment. This will create a new `run`. Within the scope of the run, we can execute the training logic.
2. Create a new for-loop to train for 10 epochs.
3. Within the for-loop, call the `train_minibatch` method on the `trainer` to train the model. Provide it a mapping between the input variables and the data to train with.
4. After this, log the `average_loss` metric for the run using the `previous_minibatch_loss_average` value from the trainer object.
5. In addition to the average loss, log the average metric in the run using the `previous_minibatch_evaluation_average` property on the trainer object.

Once we have trained the model, we can execute a test against the test set using the `test_minibatch` method. This method returns the output of the `metric` function that we created earlier. We will log this to the machine learning workspace as well.

A run allows us to keep track of data related to a single training session for a model. We can log metrics using the `log` method on the `run` object. This method accepts the name of the metric and a value for the metric. You can use this method to record things such as the output of the `loss` function to monitor how your model is converging to an optimal set of parameters.

Other things can also be logged, such as the number of epochs used to train the model, the random seed used in the program, and other useful settings that you may need in order to reproduce the experiment at a later time.

Metrics recorded during a run automatically show up on the portal when you navigate to the experiment in the machine learning workspace under the experiments tab as is shown in the image below.

Navigating to the experiment in the machine learning workspace under the experiments tab

Aside from the `log` method, there's an `upload_file` method to upload files generating during training, as demonstrated in the following code snippet. You can use this method to store model files that you've saved after training is completed:

```
z.save('outputs/model.onnx') # The z variable is the trained model
run.upload_file('model.onnx', 'outputs/model.onnx')
```

The `upload_file` method needs a name for the file, as it can be found in the workspace and a local path where the source file can be found. Please be aware of the location of the file. Due to a limitation in the Azure Machine Learning workspace, it will only pick up files from the outputs folder. This limitation will likely be lifted in the future.

Make sure you execute the `upload_file` method within the scope of the run, so that the AzureML library links the model to your experiment run as to make it traceable.

After you've uploaded the file to the workspace, you can find it in the portal under the outputs section of a run. To get to the run details, open up the machine learning workspace in Azure Portal, navigate to the experiment, and then select the run you want to see the details for as follows:

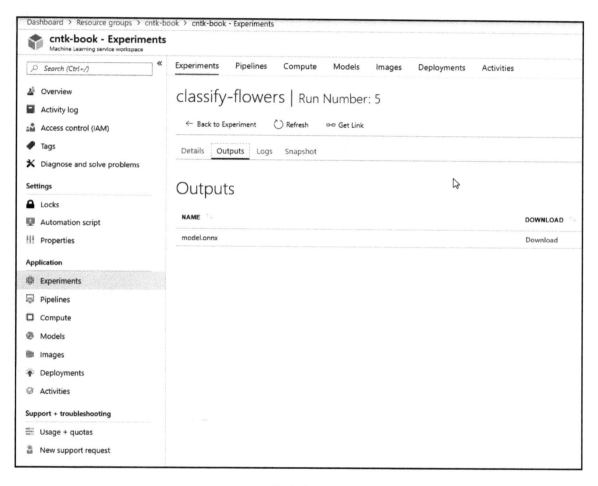

Selecting the run

Finally, when you're done with the run and want to publish the model, you can register it in the model registry as follows:

```
stored_model = run.register_model(model_name='classify_flowers',
model_path='model.onnx')
```

The `register_model` method stores the model in the model registry so you can deploy it to production. When the model was previously stored in the registry, it will automatically be stored as a new version. Now you can always go back to a previous version should you need to, as follows:

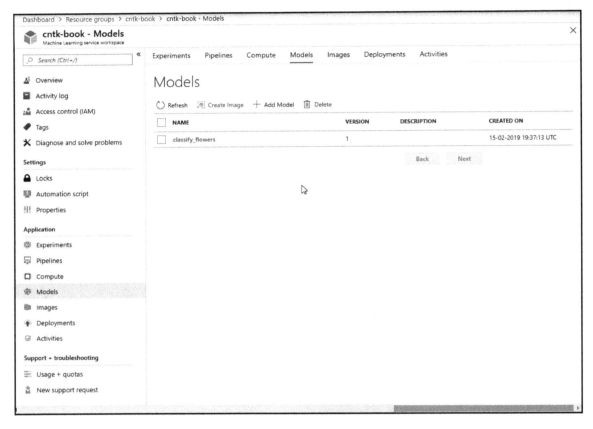

Model stored as a new version

You can find the model in the model registry in your workspace by going to the Machine Learning workspace on Azure Portal and clicking on the **Models** item in the bar in the navigation menu of the workspace.

Models are automatically related to experiment runs, so you can always find the settings that you used to train the model. This is important, as it increases the chance that you can reproduce the results, should you need to.

We've limited ourselves to running experiments locally. You can use Azure Machine Learning to run experiments on dedicated hardware, should you want to. You can read more about this on the Azure Machine Learning documentation website at: `https://docs.microsoft.com/en-us/azure/machine-learning/service/how-to-set-up-training-targets`.

Once you have completed a run for an experiment you can deploy the trained model to production. In the next section we'll explore how to do this.

Deploying your model to production

The final interesting piece of Azure Machine Learning is the deployment tooling that is included with it. The deployment tooling allows you to take a model from the model registry and deploy it to production.

Before you can deploy a model to production, you need to have an image that includes the model and a scoring script. The image is a Docker image that includes a web server, which will invoke the scoring script when a request is made against it. The scoring script accepts input in the form of a JSON payload, and uses it to make a prediction using the model. The scoring script for our iris classification model looks like this:

```
import os
import json
import numpy as np
from azureml.core.model import Model
import onnxruntime

model = None

def init():
    global model
    model_path = Model.get_model_path('classify_flowers')
    model = onnxruntime.InferenceSession(model_path)

def run(raw_data):
    data = json.loads(raw_data)
    data = np.array(data).astype(np.float32)
    input_name = model.get_inputs()[0].name
    output_name = model.get_outputs()[0].name
```

```
prediction = model.run([output_name], { input_name: data})
# Select the first output from the ONNX model.
# Then select the first row from the returned numpy array.
prediction = prediction[0][0]

return json.dumps({'scores': prediction.tolist() })
```

Follow the given steps:

1. First, import the components needed to build the script.
2. Next, define a global model variable that will contain the loaded model.
3. After that, define the init function to initialize the model in the script.
4. Within the init function, retrieve the path for the model using the `Model.get_model_path` function. This automatically locates the model file in the Docker image.
5. Next, load the model by initializing a new instance of the `onnxruntime.InferenceSession` class.
6. Define another function, `run` that accepts a single parameter `raw_data`.
7. Within the `run` function, convert the contents of `raw_data` variable from JSON to a Python array.
8. Next, convert the `data` array into a Numpy array so we can use it to make a prediction.
9. After that, use the `run` method on the loaded model and feed it the input features. Include a dictionary that tells the ONNX runtime how to map the input data to the input variable of the model.
10. The model returns an array of outputs with 1 element for the output of the model. This output contains one row of data. Select the first element from the output array and the first row from the selected output variable and store it in the `prediction` variable.
11. Finally, return the predicted output as a JSON object.

Azure Machine Learning service will automatically include any model files that you registered for a particular model when you create a container image. So, `get_model_path` will also work inside deployed images and resolve to a directory in the container that hosts the model and scoring script.

Now that we have a scoring script, let's create an image and deploy the image as a web service in the cloud. To deploy a web service, you can explicitly create an image. Or, you can let Azure Machine Learning service create one based on the configuration you provided, as follows:

```
from azureml.core.image import ContainerImage

image_config = ContainerImage.image_configuration(
    execution_script="score.py",
    runtime="python",
    conda_file="conda_env.yml")
```

Follow the given steps:

1. First, import the ContainerImage class from the `azureml.core.image` module.
2. Next, create a new image configuration using the `ContainerImage.image_configuration` method. Provide it with the score.py as the `execution_script` argument, the python `runtime` and finally provide conda_env.yml as the `conda_file` for the image.

We configure the container image to use Python as the runtime. We're also configuring a special environment file for Anaconda so that we can configure custom modules like CNTK as follows:

```
name: project_environment
dependencies:
  # The python interpreter version.
  # Currently Azure ML only supports 3.5.2 and later.
- python=3.6.2

- pip:
    # Required packages for AzureML execution, history, and data
preparation.

  - azureml-defaults
  - onnxruntime
```

Follow the given steps:

1. First, give the environment a name. This optional, but can be useful when you create an environment from this file locally for testing.
2. Next, Provide the python version 3.6.2 for your scoring script.
3. Finally, add a pip dependency to the list with a sublist containing `azureml-default` and `onnxruntime`.

The `azureml-default` package contains everything you need to work with experiments and models in the docker container image. It includes standard packages like Numpy and Pandas as well for easier installation. The `onnxruntime` package is required so we can load the model inside the scoring script that we're using.

One more step is needed to deploy the trained model as a web service. We'll need to set up a web service configuration and deploy the model as a service. Machine Learning service supports deploying to virtual machines, Kubernetes clusters, and Azure Container Instances, which are basic Docker containers running in the cloud. This is how to deploy the model to an Azure Container Instance:

```
from azureml.core.webservice import AciWebservice, Webservice

aciconfig = AciWebservice.deploy_configuration(cpu_cores=1, memory_gb=1)

service = Webservice.deploy_from_model(workspace=ws,
                                       name='classify-flowers-svc',
                                       deployment_config=aciconfig,
                                       models=[stored_model],
                                       image_config=image_config)
```

Follow the given steps:

1. First, Import the AciWebservice and Webservice classes from the azureml.core.webservice module.
2. Then, create a new `AciWebservice` configuration using the deploy_configuration method on the AziWebservice class. Provide it with a set of resource limits for the software. One CPU and 1GB of memory.
3. Once you have a configuration for the web service, deploy the model the registered model to production by calling `deploy_from_model` with the workspace to deploy from, a service name and the models that you want to deploy. Provide the image configuration you created earlier.

Once the container image is created, it will get deployed as a container instance on Azure. This will create a new resource in the resource group for your machine learning workspace.

Once the new service is started, you will see a new deployment on Azure Portal in your machine learning workspace, as seen in the following screenshot:

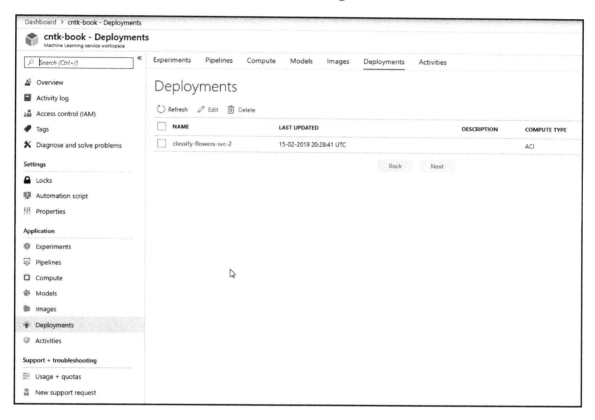

New deployment on Azure Portal in your machine learning workspace

The deployment includes a scoring URL that you can invoke from your application to use the model. Because you're using REST to invoke the model, you're isolated from the fact that it runs CNTK underneath the covers. You also have something that can be used from any programming language you can possibly think of, as long as it can execute HTTP requests.

For example, in Python, we can use the `requests` package as a basic REST client to make predictions using the service you just created. Let's start by installing the `requests` module first, as follows:

```
pip install --upgrade requests
```

With the `requests` package installed, we can write a small script to execute a request against the deployed service as follows:

```
import requests
import json

service_url = "<service-url>"
data = [[1.4, 0.2, 4.9, 3.0]]

response = requests.post(service_url, json=data)

print(response.json())
```

Follow the given steps:

1. First, import the requests and json package.
2. Next, create a new variable for the service_url and fill it with the URL for the webservice.
3. Then, create another variable, to store the data you want to make a prediction for.
4. After that, use the requests.post function to post the data to the deployed service and store the response.
5. Finally, read the JSON data returned in the response to obtain the predicted values.

The service_url can be obtained by performing the following steps:

1. First, navigate to the resource group that contains the machine learning workspace.
2. Then, select the workspace and choose the **Deployments** section on the left of the details panel.
3. Select the deployment you want to view the details of and copy the URL from the details page.

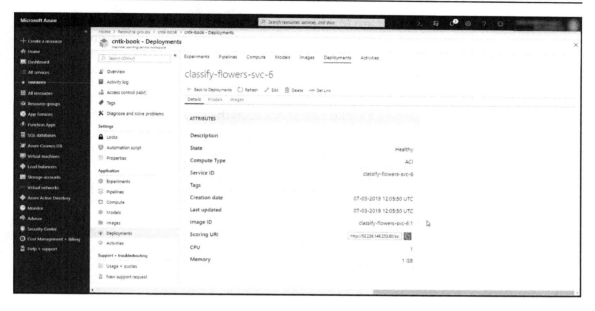

Selecting the deployment

When you run the script you just created, you'll receive a response with the predicted classes for the input sample. The output will look similar to this:

```
{"scores": [-2.27234148979187, -2.486853837966919, -0.20609207451343536]}
```

Summary

In this chapter, we've looked at what it takes to bring deep learning and machine learning models to production. We've explored some of the basic principles that will help you to be successful with deep learning in a continuous delivery environment.

We've taken a look at exporting models to ONNX to make it easier to deploy your trained models to production and keep them running for years, thanks to the portable nature of the ONNX format. We then explored how you can use the CNTK API in other languages, such as C#, to make predictions.

Finally, we've looked at using Azure Machine Learning service to level-up your DevOps experience with experiment management, model management, and deployment tools. Although you don't need a tool like this to get started, it really helps to have something like Azure Machine Learning service in your arsenal when you're planning on running a bigger project on production.

With this chapter, we've reached the end of this book. In the first chapter, we started exploring CNTK. We then looked at how to build models, feed them with data, and measure their performance. With the basics covered, we explored two interesting use cases looking at images and time series data. Finally, we ended with taking models to production. You should now have enough information get started with building your own models with CNTK!

Other Books You May Enjoy

If you enjoyed this book, you may be interested in these other books by Packt:

Deep Learning with Keras
Antonio Gulli

ISBN: 9781787128422

- Optimize step-by-step functions on a large neural network using the Backpropagation Algorithm
- Fine-tune a neural network to improve the quality of results
- Use deep learning for image and audio processing
- Use Recursive Neural Tensor Networks (RNTNs) to outperform standard word embedding in special cases
- Identify problems for which Recurrent Neural Network (RNN) solutions are suitable
- Explore the process required to implement Autoencoders
- Evolve a deep neural network using reinforcement learning

Deep Learning with PyTorch
Vishnu Subramanian

ISBN: 9781788624336

- Use PyTorch for GPU-accelerated tensor computations
- Build custom datasets and data loaders for images and test the models using torchvision and torchtext
- Build an image classifier by implementing CNN architectures using PyTorch
- Build systems that do text classification and language modeling using RNN, LSTM, and GRU
- Learn advanced CNN architectures such as ResNet, Inception, Densenet, and learn how to use them for transfer learning
- Learn how to mix multiple models for a powerful ensemble model
- Generate new images using GAN's and generate artistic images using style transfer

Leave a review - let other readers know what you think

Please share your thoughts on this book with others by leaving a review on the site that you bought it from. If you purchased the book from Amazon, please leave us an honest review on this book's Amazon page. This is vital so that other potential readers can see and use your unbiased opinion to make purchasing decisions, we can understand what our customers think about our products, and our authors can see your feedback on the title that they have worked with Packt to create. It will only take a few minutes of your time, but is valuable to other potential customers, our authors, and Packt. Thank you!

Index

regression model
    accuracy, measuring of predictions 88, 89
    performance, measuring in CNTK 90, 92
    performance, validating 88
ReLU function 40

S

small in-memory datasets
  working with 54
Stochastic Gradient Descent (SGD) 35, 149

T

TensorBoard
  using 103, 105, 106
time series data

multiple recurrent layers, training 149, 151, 152
transformations
  reference 124

U

underfitting 76

V

vanishing gradient 39

W

Windows
  Microsoft Cognitive Toolkit (CNTK), installing on
  21